A MUM LIKE THIS

A 52-week motherhood memoir

Navigating the often-contradictory world of modern motherhood

Laura Rachelle Taylor

BestPressed
- PUBLISHING -

This book is a memoir. It reflects the author's present recollections of experiences over time. Some events have been compressed and some dialogue has been recreated. All views expressed are the author's own.

ISBN: 978-1-7385015-0-2

First published by Best Pressed Publishing in 2024

Dedication and acknowledgements

For my son, Arley. Thank you for turning my mouse squeak into a lion's roar.

In loving memory of my grandma from Jack Lane. Thank you for blessing me with superpowers. Miss you every day. I see your angel messages – just as you did with your mum.

With huge high fives to Jamie. When my then-undiagnosed condition forced me to push him away, he extended his hand further and put everything aside to help. Forever Arley's hero, as well as mine.

Of course, a squillion hugs for my own mum, Beverley, for being my best friend through the highs and life coach through the lows. With never-ending talents, she even illustrated this book.

Shout-out to my soul-sister and real-life sister, Sarah, for loving us in a way I didn't know existed.

Thanks to my dad, Jim. For all the times I screamed "you're not the boss of me" – I'm sorry, boss.

My stepdad, David – thank you for driving forward with my diagnosis. I'm lucky to have you in my life.

Big thanks to the NHS, particularly our midwife, Martyne Drinkall whose warmth and kindness I will always remember. Plus, Trish Colton, our health visitor who enhanced my experience of first-time motherhood.

Not forgetting Leighton Hospital's lactation consultants, mental health midwives, and the Cherubs breastfeeding group on Facebook. Never felt so vulnerable; never felt so supported.

The team at Mrs Nursery. You consistently prove that gentleness and understanding with children, whilst flexing to support their parents, is at the heart of everything you do. I couldn't have written this book without you.

Finally, my most heartfelt middle fingers and enthusiastic V-signs all round to those who have given me unsolicited advice; judged me for breastfeeding and given me pointers on how to stop; wanted me to conform to their idea of a mum when I was doing it my way; mum-shamed me, and generally tried to make me morph into their mould. Though your commentaries have been unwelcome, you have spurred me on to write this book. Thank you.

A letter to the reader

Dear reader,

In *A Mum Like This*, I explore those special moments of early motherhood, whilst shining a spotlight on the parts that people rarely talk about. Like the idea that we should exist as everything to everyone and nobody to ourselves; that we often have to fight for our identities in a world where outdated tradition tries to make us fit a mould that no longer works; the mum-shaming; postnatal depletion, and so much more. I observe motherhood's highs, lows, science and stardust through my eyes — as someone who feels crashing lows and soars above the highest clouds of happiness with Premenstrual Dysphoric Disorder (PMDD).

Over 52 chapters – each tied up with a poem – I detail a key theme or experience from my first postpartum year. This memoir has been written in real time, during the night feeds, baby classes, dealing with motherhood meddlers and living in a garden room whilst my baby's dad built our home. It's been a journey. One I'm so proud of. Along the way, I realised that in the times that felt isolating, I wasn't alone at all. There's a wide community of mums like this, all learning to comfortably survive – and even thrive – in the often-convoluted world of modern motherhood. If you relate to this, I hope I can offer the "you're not going mad" that I could have done with.

Writing *A Mum Like This* has led me to discover that once we turn our mouse squeaks into lion's roars and push back against the unrealistic demands on our time, motherhood is filled with an even deeper level of magic than we ever could have imagined – we just have to scratch a little deeper beneath the surface to find it.

If you'd like to chat about all things parenthood or any of the themes within this book, I'd love to hear from you. I'm on Instagram: @LauraRachelleWriter.

Thanks for reading,
Laura

Contents

WEEK 1

Nesting and birthing

Never tell a pregnant woman what she wants, or that she can't do something – she has a miracle growing in her tummy.

Cravings: milk, milky buttons, milkshakes and Alan Titchmarsh. Things I'm not craving but random people are saying I should be: a dark sofa, dark walls, a PU wipeable tablecloth, carpet, and a platter of various vitamins. Why, as soon as there's mention of a baby, do our lives become a free-for-all? It feels like I'm wearing a sticker on my head that reads: "Give me advice on my body, my home, and all my personal belongings". Whilst I appreciate some of the advice, much of it is useless. I don't tell my best friend that he looks like he could do with upping his supplement intake; family friends that they've gone for the wrong colour sofa; or my Granddad that he should get his hair cut short so it's more manageable, but we're having a baby, so the microscope has turned to us. In particular, it's zoned in on me.

It's lovely in many ways. The kind and caring attention. The little window into someone's memory that they let me peer through when my rounded tummy has reminded them of a magical segment of their pregnancy or early parenthood. I love the way this experience opens a new world of conversations; it deepens my relationship with many people. My Venn diagram of friends and acquaintances has become more diverse and interesting, even before I've had the baby. In the next moment, some of the "do this, do that and just you wait"s – mostly from random people – are sending me into a spin. There are so many pieces of unsolicited advice which, as a newly first-time pregnant person, I feel inclined to listen to. I've never had a human in my tummy before so, erm, help, but the sudden explosion of advice is overwhelming.

All the tips seem to butt heads with each other, leaving me in the middle feeling confused, whilst also coursing with happy hormones that make me the most elated and excited I've ever been – despite having my head down the toilet for most of my sickly pregnant life so far. What a contradictory little happy-scared bubble this is. I've a feeling the misplaced comments will gather momentum as time goes by and once my baby is born, will shoot out with more force than I worry he will (spoiler from the future: I did not need to worry about that). These self-assumed interior designers, midwives and doctors will no doubt graduate, in their minds, to architects and paediatric nurses once our baby is here.

Most of the comments are about my decor choices. "Your home won't be white and clean forever", is the biggest mistruth I've heard. "Just you wait! As soon as that baby arrives, you'll be desperate for some dark colours, and you'll wish you never bought that cream sofa". That cream sofa. Who knew that buying a sofa could become local headline news? Once that embryo is ticking over in your tummy, your sofa, hair product, and chosen drinking vessel, is apparently everyone's business. Another note from the future, as I edit this book: the cream sofa still looks great, even after a house move and living in a shed with a baby for the best part of a year. Never tell a pregnant woman what she wants, or that she can't do something – she has a miracle growing in her tummy.

Meddlers aside, I've never felt happier than in these last few weeks of pregnancy. I'm glad I've given myself time, space, and grace for nesting, plus a healthy dollop of blissful ignorance and self-indulgence. Instinctively, I knew that these would be the last few weeks and days to soak up life without the responsibilities that come with having a baby-sized shadow. I've blocked out my calendar with the note: "Me time – nesting", to make sure I don't find myself amidst a flurry of "normal world" plans, when really all I want to do is embrace this special, anticipatory period of my life. This is the perfect excuse to revel in my solitude. It's a couple of weeks before our due date and I'm on maternity leave with no plans with anyone except myself and my fiancé, Jamie.

At home, the naps are never-ending and guilt-free. White, soft, calm. That's the setup I've created through my interiors. I'm a nester by nature and have always enjoyed interior styling. Since going into some form of turbo-power nesting mode on maternity leave, my home is in full bloom. Every corner of my perfectly manicured den has been cleaned, considered, and styled with the comfortable, cosy fabrics I've been craving. Some call it impressive, others call it over the top, I call it home.

It's November and I've taken my home-making efforts up a notch by creating a hygge-inspired winter grotto in my living room, filled with my favourite colour of all: warm white Christmas lights. Let the festive films roll. I watch them in my cinnamon-spice-scented lounge, with marshmallow-and-cream hot chocolates resting on my bump. I delight in watching the chocolate ripple in the mug as my baby kicks and twirls in my tummy. Thankfully, my waters broke on the old sofa. The cream one came afterwards.

When Time Stood Still

This is the time
The first few precious hours
This is the moment
We'll talk about
Forever

Nine months waiting
Wondering who you'll be
Now journeying through labour
Before this wait will be over
And they'll hand you to me

Each contraction brings us closer
You're finally on your way
The excitement of every kick and heartbeat
Now I'm elated and exhausted
And excited and supported
Yet
Afraid

The minutes are turning to hours
The hours are turning to days
And now I feel the urge
To push
This
Long
Labour
Away

Pushing and pushing
But this isn't meant to be
Doctors scramble around
A rush to theatre
Hurry! hurry!

Then, after the fuss
The moment when your world
Finally
Collides with mine
Raising your arm in the air as they lift you out
Victory!
But
They haven't handed you to me

"Look over the sheet", says the doctor
"He's on his way over"
Now the chatter muffles to silence
As I glimpse your purple body being carried away
On a surgeon's shoulder

Time stood still as we wonder
What this ending will be?
Will the mood turn sombre or –
Will we celebrate
Two becoming three?

Footsteps
Hushed voices
Sounds like I'm underwater
I hear the ticking of the clock

Tick tock

But time seems
To have
Stopped

Tick
Tick
Tick
…Tock?

Then the silence merges
Into tiny cries

That's him
He's alive!

Still fighting my closing eyes
Though I really need to rest
But here's the moment
We'll talk about forever
You're finally on my chest

Like a tiny baby frog
Out sticks each little leg
I observe your wrinkles of skin
Like a baby salamander
You haven't grown into it yet

Your hair curls around your ear like a miniature elf
Didn't realise babies were born this small
Your features are so tiny
But with these never-ending legs
You're bound to be tall

When time stood still
I've never felt so detached from the world
We're watching life through a bubble
Everything else
On hold

These are the moments I'll treasure
When time stood still
These are the memories
We'll talk about
Forever.

WEEK 2

That certain shade of blue

There's nothing glamorous about this and it feels hard, yet I find myself revelling in this series of special moments.

All that fuss about the cream sofa – which arrived a couple days after my baby did – and I've still not had the pleasure of sinking into it. My boys lounge back like the kings of the castle, whilst I'm squirming around on the floor like a poorly worm. I'd been so excited to do a post-birth running jump and starfish on the bed face-first but, though my life is currently filled with joy, that's one joyful moment that hasn't happened yet. Fair play to the "don't be upset if your labour doesn't go as imagined" tip. I indeed hadn't imagined labouring for so long, or to have stitches across my swollen lower stomach, which sting in harmony with the contractions that I thought would be over by now. Apparently, this is my womb contracting back into place, ushered along by each breastfeed. No one warns you of this post-labour continuation of labour, do they? Good job I received all those warnings about the cream sofa, though…

After those few days of labouring, pushing, having a temporary sunroof made for my baby to pop out of, then being stitched up again, my body doesn't seem to know how to work anymore. I thought I'd breeze out of Leighton Hospital looking all polished like Princess Kate did. I'd planned the most beautiful dress to wear for my "hi, I'm a mum now" moment. Instead, I shuffled out in a sick-strewn hoodie and leggings, accessorised with an air of Frankenstein's monster about me.

I can't feel my stomach muscles, so I need to be lifted out of bed by Jamie, who also hands our baby to me for each feed during the day and night. I still haven't been for that famous post-birth number two – should I be worried? – but despite being carried to the toilet where Jamie props my feet up on a Christmas present box (whilst delivering a fascinating but poorly-timed monologue about how cavemen used to poo), I'm completely distracted by this new life before me. There's nothing glamorous about this and it feels hard, yet I find myself revelling in this series of special moments.

My cloudy brain is peppered with funny little thoughts about birth. Do you ever have those useless, yet weirdly satisfying mind take-overs? My pre-pregnancy brain used to be full of them. *If a room is painted many times, over and over again, does the space inside the room eventually become so small that it closes up? If you cut through it, would it be a beautiful cross-section of colours, like a layer cake?* This time, I'm thinking along the lines of: *I wonder how my insides looked when they were splayed out on an operating table? Wonder if any of the outside world, like the surgeon's eyelash, got left in my womb? Did I get a decent enough look at my placenta?* Welcome to the mind of a detailed thinker.

Midwives come and go in a flurry of caring smiles, heel prick tests, weighing scales and tears. *Many, many* tears. I cry into the arms of a few comforting ladies wearing NHS lanyards. I sob into the embrace of Trish, our health visitor who even wrote my shopping list and dropped my baby's GP enrolment form at the doctors for me. Our family is a great source of emotional and physical help, but there's a certain kind of comfort to be found in a lady wearing an NHS lanyard. They feel like part of my family and I don't want them to leave. The moment I see that comforting shade of NHS blue, I feel happily overwhelmed with the flurry of love around me.

Our NHS midwives and health visitors are the picket fence to my little newborn nest. They're not paid enough to fulfil the duty of care that they carry out so well. Each one I meet becomes a counsellor, a helpful voice in the newborn haze, a fleeting friend. Inside my nest, I've been propped up with various pillows like a queen bee. Time seems to have stood still again for a few days whilst the world continues to buzz along outside.

Since I mentioned breastfeeding had become painful, helpful lactation consultants in NHS lanyards have been over to offer support, "check the latch", as seems to be the popular phrase, or show me how to use a breast pump. I asked a consultant to take a picture of my baby's now-perfect latch that she orchestrated, so I could copy it later. I thought breastfeeding would be as simple as putting the baby to your chest and milk comes out. That's how it seems to happen with the sheep and their lambs on Alan Titchmarsh's Sunday morning programmes. I didn't realise that an awkward latch could make things so tricky, so I'm capturing this "tummy to Mummy" skill in photographic form. Jamie's practical-minded skillset later comes in useful again, as it turns out he can arrange our baby's tiny bird-like body just right. He didn't even have to scroll through my – in hindsight, quite bizarre – photoshoot that the nurse took for me, to recreate that hold.

So that's how we're muddling through these early days of non-stop feeding. Did you know, a newborn's tummy is around the size of a marble? [1] That's why they need to feed so often.

Night Feeds Whilst the World Sleeps

I watch your tummy going up and down
As you sleep across my chest
I should put you back in your cot
But I steal a few moments more
Though my back is sore
Tummy is on fire
Stitches sting
I miss lying on my side
Cuddling Dad
Starfishing

Here, we lie half-awake for hours in the night
Soaking in each sweet second of this alone time
It won't last forever
So, we crank the blinds to look at the stars
You nestle your tiny, dimpled hands in mine
Bedside snacks
Pillow den built high
Me and you next to your dad
Our time

The silence is punctuated by your gasps and gulps
You pull back to stare at me
Breaking into a sweet smile
Then guzzle again
After bobbing your mouth side to side
Hungry-fish style

It'd be easy to complain
I'm tired
I feel far from who I used to be
I'm drained
But look how lucky we are

I've lost myself for now
Yet
Look how much I've gained.

WEEK 3

The people-pleasing begins

"Do this and do that but don't do anything at all". This is exactly how it feels when I listen to the trash spoken by the small segment of society that I've come to know as "the motherhood meddlers".

I'm letting the exhaustion and fluctuating emotions of new motherhood swirl me around without resistance. This life feels miles apart from the one I knew last month, but it's the most wholesome kind of chaos. One aspect I'm not enjoying so much is the contradictory comments, which are coming in thick and fast. It's irritating. My motherly instincts confirm that I don't need any of these clashing opinions but of course, the new mum must always be polite and smile. Society expects it. It seems that a new mother is almost always required to respond to nonsensical "advice" with elegance when she'd no doubt prefer to elegantly unfurl her middle finger. Or maybe that's just me.

As predicted in week one, the self-assumed interior designers, midwives and doctors did indeed graduate, in their minds, to architects and paediatric nurses after the birth. I've even come across self-appointed baby fashion stylists ("what *has* your mummy dressed you in?") I find myself trying to gauge what kind of mum I'm expected to be in whoever's company we find ourselves in, just to make my life temporarily easier whilst I juggle all the balls of new motherhood. Nothing about this feels healthy for my brain. The comments in themselves are harmless and probably just an awkward filler to follow "what a beautiful boy". Still, the sudden onset of strange and invasive statements that seem to form society's template reaction to a new human entering the world, is exhausting. I've never heard so many overbearing sentences – or seen so many people – in such a short period of time, in my life. This all feels too much for my ambivert personality type.

Jamie is an amazing gatekeeper and I don't know how I'd get through this crazy phase without him turning visitors away from time to time, but we're still coming up against challenges we never could have planned for, like texts, which we don't have the time to check right now, telling us – rather than asking us – that we have visitors on their way. I've been advised by midwives and health visitors to surround myself with a small but strong support network, happy programmes, and a stress-free, calm atmosphere to encourage the release of oxytocin, which helps to supply a steady flow of breastmilk for my baby. Whilst I'd love to do that, I find that with the flurry of visitors and clashing opinions and personalities, it's near impossible to police what and who I surround myself with.

Though my soft, calm nest at home provides the perfect backdrop for relaxation, I often find myself engaging in a whirlwind of plans to see my baby, annoying questions – are they really annoying, or is this my hormones? Nobody knows – and people clamouring to come round. I'm temporarily moulding myself into someone else, purely just to get others off my back. I find myself wondering: *Is this person all for holding my baby whilst he naps, or should I put him down in his cot? I'd like to hold him, but this visitor has already made "aren't you going to put him down?" comments.* At the moment, I'm too depleted to deal with even the mildest and most well-meaning confrontations regarding mothering choices. I'd rather simply mould into the woman I'm expected to be, until I feel strong enough to be myself again. So here I am, people-pleasing my way through visits.

Nonsensical comments would usually go over my head, but new motherhood feels like a vulnerable place, both mentally and physically. I'm still healing from the birth. My brain has no extra room for simple concepts like benefit of the doubt, reason, or logic. Even jokes are lost on me at the moment. The only intuition I have is linked to the way I mother my baby and even that still gets knocked over sometimes. Things that once came naturally to me, now seem hard. I realise that, in the midst of this time, those whose support extends beyond the newborn cuddles, are thriving in their care for us; they've seemingly moulded their love into a new shape that I didn't know we needed. With these people, I feel safe and comfortable in the knowledge that I don't need to understand their jokes, adapt my mothering choices, wipe toothpaste from around my mouth, or host them. Others are adding nothing but unnecessary pressure at a time when we need nothing but support.

With those who are adding pressure, I'm changing tact, as I begin to crave time with no visitors at all. I feel myself slowly withdrawing from this world of contradictory comments. It's too draining when you're so fresh into new motherhood, to juggle other people and their expectations when you're also nurturing a human that you just baked for nine months. In particular, I'm wriggling from the mould of expectations that I'm apparently now obliged to crawl into. "You started off so well, ironing all his sleepsuits before he was born. What happened? You're a mum now and can't cherry pick the best bits!" Actually, I can and I will pick whichever cherries look the most delicious. *Schlurp ← note to reader: that's the sound of me, munching through those delicious cherries*. We read books, play my weird and wonderful made-up games, and do anything and everything that doesn't involve an ironing board. These days are precious.

With time, I'd like to find my strength and confidence again and create a comfortable enough distance to ensure I no longer soak up and suck in the nonsensical comments. I'm working towards looking down on each one from above – acknowledging its existence, yet not paying it any attention. These remarks don't deserve the time or attention I'm giving them. "Do this and do that but don't do anything at all". This is exactly how it feels when I listen to the trash spoken by the small segment of society that I've come to know as "the motherhood meddlers".

Mum-Shaped Shoes to Fill

Bring him here
We don't see him enough
But take him away
That screaming is rough
Put him down
You're holding him too much
But don't put him down
He needs his mother's touch
Don't forget to burp him
He needs more patting on the back
And what about the swaddling?
I see a distinct lack of that
Design him a fancy nursery
I can't wait to see what you do!
Except, babies don't use nurseries
He needs to be attached to you!
So, make sure you breastfeed
But don't feed around me
I find that so disgusting
When I'm
Asleep
Awake

Or drinking tea
Sleep when he sleeps
But get that washing done
And don't forget to iron those sleepsuits
Every
Single
One
Thought about stopping breastfeeding?
Might make him sleep through the night
Oh, I'm judging everything you do but
None of it will ever be right
You need to heal
Get plenty of rest
But never fall asleep
Because
Shouldn't you be
Washing
Tidying
Hosting
Cooking
Working
Socialising
And feathering the nest?
I know you've just given birth
But he hasn't met any of my friends?
Bring him here before you think
Of spending time alone with him again
Snuggle all day on the sofa
He needs to feel you there
But don't ever stay in the house
Babies need play dates
Cuddles with strangers
Expensive baby groups
To be kept awake
Feeds
But not by you
First-class entertainment and fresh air
When are you going back to work?
Don't forget about your career

But don’t miss a single second
Of baby's first few years
What’s that?
You have needs, too?
Probably should have thought about that
Before having a baby
Shouldn’t you?
Eat whilst baby feeds
But always answer the door
You need to take in the neighbour's parcels
Isn't that what your maternity leave is for?
You'll snap back into shape
I'm quite sure of that
But how come you haven't?
You'll never get your figure back
Oh, darling
Now you've lost weight?
You look tired?
Actually
You're looking really ill
Please get yourself back on track
You have mum-shaped shoes to fill.

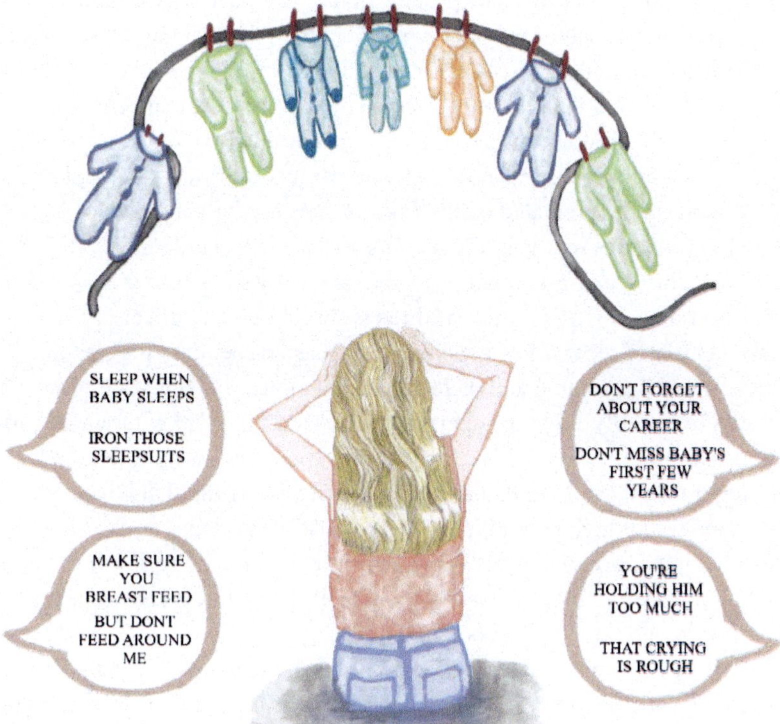
SLEEP WHEN BABY SLEEPS
IRON THOSE SLEEPSUITS
MAKE SURE YOU BREAST FEED
BUT DONT FEED AROUND ME
DON'T FORGET ABOUT YOUR CAREER
DON'T MISS BABY'S FIRST FEW YEARS
YOU'RE HOLDING HIM TOO MUCH
THAT CRYING IS ROUGH

WEEK 4

Trusting my instincts

I might not be the smiling, people-pleasing "of course you can!" person who I once was anymore, but I honestly wouldn't have it any other way.

I sit on the floor, tightly clutching my four-week-old as I watch the clashing scenes above us through the reflection in his eyes. Joyful Christmas lights are dancing beneath the blue flash of ambulance beacons. Gift bags litter the path of medical bags. A stretcher sits on top of Christmas stockings. These disjointed visuals remind me of a Photoshopped version of the *Girl with a Pearl Earring* I once saw. In the modernised iteration of this historic masterpiece, the girl originally painted in 1665 wearing a gold turban, was now depicted in a backless top, denim shorts and Converse. It fascinated me because of how bonkers it looked – a crossing of worlds that would never normally brush shoulders.

Like a disco at a funeral or a stripper at a baby shower, our first Christmas evening as a family of three is serving up an unlikely combination of scenes. Festive excitement has crashed into pure panic. We're away from home and there's been a serious accident which was out of our control. My foggy postpartum mind hadn't kept up with whose turn it was to hold my newborn. He's safe but I've spent one seemingly never-ending moment thinking that my baby was involved and that he and someone we all love very much, had been badly harmed – or worse. Following those moments of worry, my limbs felt like they didn't fit together properly anymore, as a prickly feeling of panic swept to the ends of my fingers and toes. Time stood still again.

Even as I sit with my boy back in my arms, the words being spoken around me are blurring into a thick, sticky, swirling acrylic painting. Van Gogh's *Starry Night* with a touch of Picasso's *The Weeping Woman.* I note the way these moments of unexpected panic have ramped up since I became a mum, as I cuddle my baby so closely that the weave of my jovial Christmas snowman jumper has imprinted into his skin. It feels like I'm about to sick my heart up and out of my chest, and my mind is drowning in that unhelpful yet all-consuming thought that seems to go together with moments that feel traumatic: *What if?* As a mum, all I can think about is what I could have done better to protect my baby. We'd accepted an offer of help and started to relax, unaware that this alcohol-led accident was unravelling outside of our newborn bubble. *Should I have been paying closer attention to what was happening around me? Was I wrong to relax for a moment?* Being on the high-level of alert required by new-motherhood feels almost impossible when my body is recovering and I haven't slept – all whilst the impacts of breastfeeding continue to make me feel drained and emotionally disorientated. This is hard and my brain has no room left for anything beyond keeping my baby alive. I'm craving the comfort and safety of home.

Accident aside, being away from home feels unnatural anyway. I've been trying to socialise and hold conversations whilst my womb is still contracting back into place. I'm often grasping my own hand in a futile attempt to expel the shooting pains that launch through my lower abdomen before seeping into my legs. The postpartum blood flow is showing no signs of slowing down and I keep checking everywhere I've been sitting to make sure I haven't bled on someone else's sofa. At home, I sat on postpartum bed mats, but it seemed neither festive nor socially acceptable to bring them along for our Christmas celebrations.

I've found it hard to act "normal" when I feel anything but normal. Even so, it's Christmas, so me and my sore, leaky boobs are – or were – determined to socialise and enjoy ourselves. In the pauses that haven't been consumed by discomfort, I've been leaving the room to peer down my absorbent postpartum *Bridget Jones* knickers, as I check that my C-section stitches are still intact. The slightest movement offsets a stinging pain which has me convinced that the stitches have come away and my stomach is gaping open. Each time, I'm surprised to see that they're still as they should be, but in this state of intense vulnerability, I just want to be looked after at home.

I underestimated how hard I'd find it to deal with the tricky postpartum cocktail of emotions, bodily fluids, hormones, and protective instincts whilst I'm away from my own surroundings. We're still in the newborn bubble and I need my calm, chaos-free nest. *Home, home, home.* That's all I can think about. I'm desperate to return to the cosiness I'd created there so I can focus on caring for my baby, distraction-free. This is my maternal nesting instinct in its full protective force, and I take a moment to appreciate how clever this is. Welcoming a baby is one key time in our lives when we need uncompromised peace and protection. Our animal instincts call for a place that allows us to focus on keeping our offspring alive whilst we're at our most depleted. Plus, feeling comfy and protected encourages that milk-flow-maximising oxytocin, which if breastfeeding, helps to keep our babies fed, as Trish the health visitor reminds me. Back in caveman times, a safe space to nurture a baby was a life-or-death scenario. Create a secure base to raise your little one or face attack from a bear. Simple as that. Though evolution has come a long way since then, I appreciate these old-as-time instincts that led me to fill my home with comfort and safety. I embrace the motherly intuition that's telling me to take my baby back to our newborn bubble, inside our cosy, cinnamon-scented nest that we call home.

It's a few hours later and we're finally home, though the cinnamon fragrance is overpowered by the scent of upset that's seeped into the fabric of the clothes we've been wearing over the last couple of days. I'm eager to remove it from the house, so I wash and pack away our outfits, including my baby's "My First Christmas" sleepsuits. I imagined these would be stored as festive-time treasure in our memory box. In reality, I never want to see or smell them again, so I'm donating them to charity. I feel traumatised by the strange mix of festivities and panic. Even the exhausted look of upset that's etched into Jamie's face unsettles me. I wonder if other new parents would feel and respond in the same way. Our baby is unharmed, but the mere thought of him being injured feels too much to process. This must be a trauma response.

Trauma is a topic I'm fascinated by. Whether it's caused by prolonged suffering or a short moment of panic, I've heard it said before that experiences we find traumatic, add extra sensitivity to the brain's in-built emotional alarm system, known as the amygdala[2]. Evidently, this clever danger alert often becomes more reactive after a bad experience, to prevent anything similar from happening again. Meanwhile, the brain's in-built comfort blanket, known as the prefrontal cortex, is said to become less sensitive after a trauma. It's not as ready and willing to wrap us in the "it's okay" cocoon, after something we perceive as scary has happened – because it's not sure if it will be okay. It's clever, really.

The sensitised amygdala and desensitised prefrontal cortex both help to protect us against future dangers. When we do come up against a similar situation, it can send the human fight-or-flight response into overdrive, meaning we tend to get pretty anxious in similar scenarios. During the second or so that I spent thinking my baby had been harmed, I could almost feel those trauma response changes re-wiring my brain, as I made a slow-motion mental note to never push my motherly instincts aside in favour of people-pleasing again. Amidst the relief of having him back in my arms, I can tell I've been equipped with a stronger level of protection than before. On the horizon, there's a swirling hurricane of torturous thoughts ready to suck me in, but what good will that do?

Instead of dwelling on the negatives, I flood my mind with thoughts of those special, anticipatory days before my little one arrived. I'll forever treasure the memories of that season, like snuggling into blankets in my winter nest as I devoured endless Christmas films and hot chocolates. I loved watching the marshmallows dancing in my mug as my baby kicked it from inside my tummy. Not forgetting the warming voice of Alan Titchmarsh, or the magic and excitement of Christmas Eve at my mum's, where we snuggled beside the Christmas tree with our new little love, waiting for Santa to arrive. Happy memories.

I've even begun to summon a level of gratitude for the events that followed those magical moments. The accident confirmed a profound lesson that prior to parenthood, I hadn't yet learned: just like labour and birth, no matter how much you meticulously plan for something, life can always throw a curveball – and that's okay. It's not down to me to feel guilty about things that are out of my control. I can only control how *I* respond and move forward. That moment of trauma needs to be about learning, re-addressing my motherhood boundaries and continuing my life with love. I swap any feelings of negativity for being calm, happy, and present with my son.

Closing my eyes, I take one deep breath and reset. This unsettling Christmas has given me a confidence boost when it comes to trusting my instincts. As a new mum, it's easy to get sucked into ensuring everyone has their fair share of newborn cuddles. For some reason, I felt compelled to make sure each person had quality time with my boy, without me watching on like a proud spare part. Nobody else made me feel that way – these feelings were self-imposed and I have no idea where they stemmed from, but this has been the turning point I needed. From now on, my son's needs and my motherly instincts are at the heart of every decision I make. It seems I'm not alone on this journey of self-discovery.

Editing this book from the future, every mum I've formed a friendship with has told me of their struggles to assert their boundaries in favour of people-pleasing. It's a lesson we all seem to learn – and often benefit from – somewhere along the road; I just learned it a little earlier than my friends. Some of us start off as these awkward little caterpillars, slithering along a recovery journey whilst keeping a baby alive and trying to make ourselves smaller and less of an inconvenience; then we grow into blossoming, confident butterflies with unshakeable boundaries.

I might not be the smiling, people-pleasing "of course you can!" person who I once was anymore, but I honestly wouldn't have it any other way. Ultimately, I'm thankful for this experience. It feels like life threw bricks at us during a time when my baby and I needed extra bricks around us, but we caught each one and built a fortress. There's no room in my new-mum heart for negativity, so I close the book on that chapter and turn my attention to my baby. I spend wholesome time with our new family of three, finding contentment in the simplicity of life at home – in the peaceful, cosy nest that I'd made during my maternity leave. I watch my son as he lies next to me. Milk-drunk and happy, he darts his almond-shaped eyes around with no real purpose. This is the start of our journey. There's a whole map waiting to be explored and I feel both blessed and excited to see life through his innocent eyes as he continues to grow.

Innocent Eyes

Startle reflex
Little sparrow thighs
Sleeping, mostly
Then I'm blessed with a glance
From those innocent eyes

Here's the start of our journey
The map is untouched
We're focused on basics:
Feeding, cuddling
Warmth and love

Yet bundled before me in a blanket
Lies a whole new world
I'll see life through magical lenses
Where the ordinary sparkles

And stillness dances and twirls
Where woodland animals talk
And wash-out days are whimsical
Where there's fun to be found in nature
Joy and excitement
Will be typical

No over-analysis
No mental paralysis
Just an endless blend of colour
Animation
Imagination
Happiness

In December, we'll make traditions
Waiting for Santa to arrive
As the warmth of Christmas lights
Reflect sparkling magic
In innocent eyes

Birthdays will become a celebration again
No more "oh, it's just another year"
There'll be a buzz amidst us
Because we'll have our family
Our little person here

Where we once rolled our eyes
At kids knocking at the door
Now we'll answer it with enthusiasm
Because it's Halloween
And this is what we dressed up for

I've no time for drama
My once wide-open heart has closed
It's wrapped around the new life before me
With space only for the wholesome love
The kind that encompasses us both

So, if anybody needs me
I’ll be over here, mesmerised
Rediscovering life
Through the magic
Of innocent eyes.

WEEK 5

Teenager, take two

I'm luxuriating in the long nights ahead of me, watching programmes I never got around to before, through half-open, hazy eyes as I feed my baby until I hear the birds' morning song.

These newborn days remind me of being young and carefree. What's carefree about having a life depend upon you? Nothing. But I'm finding that it comes with a licence to forget about social norms and throw adulthood out of the window, in many ways. You can fight the loss of your normal routine – or embrace it. I've chosen to let the ebbs and flows of motherhood sweep me up and swish me around in whichever direction they choose. I slink into my nightie with more slinkiness than before and I'm just about starting to enjoy the comfort of our much-talked-about sofa now that my stitches sting less. I sink into it with a little more "ahh" than I would have done before I became a mum.

I'm luxuriating in the long nights ahead of me, watching programmes I never got around to before, through half-open, hazy eyes as I feed my baby until I hear the birds' morning song. The skylarks and song thrushes have become my pleasant new alarm clock. Their comforting whistles signal that it's almost time to switch from pyjamas to day clothes. Not because I'm going anywhere; I still can't drive because of my C-section wound and I'm too happily exhausted to leave the house anyway. I'm continuing with the same "feed-nap-nappy-change" routine, so the uniform doesn't matter. Even so, grabbing a ten-second shower and slipping into something daytime-ish helps me to feel grounded. Plus, it's always nice to smell good for whoever's delivering the post today. When it's the postlady, her pleasant presence lingers longer than usual and I enjoy our chats. I never had the time to be carefree and conversational when I was on the hamster wheel of work, work, work, repeat.

Having a licence to forget about routines and work makes me feel like a teenager, minus the mini dress and heels. Teenager, take two. This version of teenage-hood might come with a life depending upon me, but it's also accompanied by a sense of relief about not having to look at my phone, not needing to be in the loop with work, and not needing to be generally in the know about anything. I've grown tired of being "in touch" with the world and wish I could stay in this detached state forever. Ignorance is indeed bliss. Everyone knows I'm busy, so I have a free pass to ignore the snowstorm of texts and WhatsApp messages – for now.

My body isn't feeling hungover from a night out. It's battered from birth so this time, I will soak up the sympathy. Plus, I won't sleep even if I do go to bed on time, so I'll watch as much TV as I like. After five weeks of going completely cold turkey on Alan Titchmarsh, I've rediscovered him. It turns out, whether I'm pregnant or not, I find him to be a very comforting man. Now, alongside *Love Your Weekend,* I'm watching *Gardeners' World* and *Love Your Garden* on repeat– alongside *JosieLdn* on YouTube. Josie's gardening vlogs are pure comfort in video form. When I'm feeling overwhelmed, her herbaceous border never lets me down. I love being given the time, space, and grace to enjoy this episode of my life. May as well be comfortable whilst I'm on-call for my baby, so these programmes become the comforting underscore to my hazy brain.

I think about what will be happening in my world of routine. It'll be the Friday meeting at work now. *I wonder how those projects are going?* Meanwhile, I'm taking my baby for a walk, embracing this new slow-yet-fast, relaxed-yet-full-on pace of life. This time, the distance of my walk isn't measured in minutes or miles; it's measured in the time it takes for my baby to fall asleep or signal that he's ready for a feed. Though tricky at times, one day I'll reflect on this season like I do on my teenage-hood: I'm not sure how I stayed out partying as a teenager and still made it to work the next day, but I did, and I wore it like a badge of honour. This is how I'm getting through these days, embracing this beautiful season and giving myself metaphorical high-fives as I make it through another sleepless night, fuelled by love. One day I'll miss this newborn haze.

The Newborn Haze

No more office spreadsheets
Postpartum blood on bedsheets

No sleep
No need
Drained and recharged by this baby in front of me

Taking this blissful limbo in

Not sure what our new “real life” will bring

Embracing the ignorance of not knowing
Miracles are all my tired eyes are showing

Pregnancy, birth, early motherhood
They knocked me over
They built me up

Body broken
Life made
Crazy times, these newborn days

No more making plans for a while
Time speeds past in sleeps
Cries
Smiles

Forget checking the time
It’s measured in nappy changes, feeds
How many times the postlady popped by

No checking WhatsApp
They know I’m focussed on endless cuddles and catnaps

Still feeling phantom baby kicks
The flutters, punches
Braxton Hicks

No more weird cravings going on
(Though I’ve still got Alan Titchmarsh on)

Night feeds feeling lonely
Anyone out here with me?

The cuteness of newborn babygrows
Happy sobs at sleeping eyes
Sweet button nose

Forgiven for forgetting responsibilities this time
Balancing the challenges of keeping a baby alive

Life changed
In so many ways

How
I
Love
This newborn haze.

WEEK 6

Science and stardust

Though our physical umbilical cord has been cut, it seems to have left an indelible mark inside the souls of us both.

I never anticipated the pull I'd feel towards my baby. Before I became a mum, I didn't understand why parents fussed over their offspring so obsessively. It feels strange to reflect on that thought process. Birth has rewired my brain in many ways. Prior to experiencing this bond, I thought I'd be keen to hand him over to his grandparents so I could get a segment of myself back. It hasn't been like that at all. I crave time with him, even when he's in another room. My sense of self is on hold for now and I'm at peace with that whilst this never-ending yet short season speeds by. Everyone's insistent on reminding me that if I blink, I'll miss it – so pass me the matchsticks. I'm here to soak up every second.

Evidently, my baby feels the same strong attachment to me. I see it on his face when he's carried around a crowded room. His almond-shaped eyes get wider and his mouth forms a thoughtful "O" shape until we're reunited and he clasps onto my clothing that bit tighter. I wonder how it must feel for him, having so many new faces, places, and concepts to get used to. The simplest details must seem strange, like air conditioning against his skin, a world of new textures, bright lights and rooms of muffled chatter. Even when I'm deep in conversation and don't have my eyes on my son, I feel the maternal pull when he's carried a few steps too far away. Though our physical umbilical cord has been cut, it seems to have left an indelible mark inside the souls of us both. Its physical presence has metamorphosed into a strong bond and now we both feel the tension when we're separated by more than a couple of metres. When the tension pulls too tight, it's either his cry or my instinct to bring him close that ensures we ping back together

I wonder if we'll remain close when he's a grown man. I wouldn't expect to be as close as we are now – of course he will form his own relationships beyond me and I'll make sure I continue to build my own life beyond him – but I hope that whenever he needs or misses me, he'll return home for a catch-up and still feel this same sense of love and care. No doubt this invisible umbilical cord will grow and change alongside his needs as he gets older; I'll be here to support that in whichever shape or form he needs.

It's magical when you think about how the umbilical cord works. Crafted from a flurry of science and stardust, its formation begins during the embryonic stage of pregnancy, which starts at around week three of gestation. By week seven, the cord is fully formed, including the umbilical vein, which carries oxygen and nutrients from the placenta to the foetus[3]. How clever is that? I wonder if the umbilical cord's tangible presence really can metamorphose into the bond that we share in the outside world? I feel blessed to have this connection with my baby. I know parents experience varying levels of bonding and I'll never lose sight of how lucky we are to feel so close in these early days.

Invisible Umbilical Cord

Our eyes lock together as you're carried around a crowded room
I note the worry across your face
Because you're used to being held in my arms
In the warmth and comfort of my womb

Your cosy water den has transformed from darkness
Into a world exploding with colour, people and light
There are a million things you don't understand yet
Like the difference between day and night

You're being whisked through a world
So far from what you've known
New places, faces, spaces
Not what you recognise as "home"

I want to remind them that you've never felt a draft before
Or seen the blinding brightness of the sun
You've never been lost in a crowd of faces
Or felt hunger in your tum

We're detached from our physical umbilical cord now
This invisible one is much longer

And now that you're in the outside world
The elasticity is much stronger

This love stems so far beyond
Anything I've ever known
You search for me because
I'm your comfort blanket
Your entire world
Your home

So, the further you're carried away
The tighter this cord will pull
Until we snap back together
And my heart
Once again
Is full

I feel an immense pressure to share you
Equally
With everyone
But Mum and baby have a special bond
We're attached by an invisible umbilical cord
So, for now
We only come as one.

WEEK 7

First time on our own

We're weaving our way through a series of small seasons that disappear as fast as they came, morphing into something new each time.

Welcome to my debut day of being a fully-fledged grown-up. Over the past six weeks, we've been lucky to have had supportive friends and family fluttering in and out to check on us. It's week seven and the visitors have faded. Though I enjoyed having people here, I'm loving the freedom of having space to explore motherhood on my own. I've de-Christmassed my home to mark the end of the festive season, noting how much has happened in my life since I nested in my winter grotto. It's been a wonderfully wild few weeks and now it's time for Jamie's full return to work after a staggered paternity leave and Christmas. I hear the once-familiar sound of his van leaving the drive, except this time, I listen to its low rumble with a baby in my arms. I'm nervous but excited as my little one and I find ourselves navigating another unknown phase of this journey we're on. We're weaving our way through a series of small seasons that disappear as fast as they came, morphing into something new each time.

Now, we have yet another whole new world to adjust to: the world of pure, undiluted motherhood. I'm solo parenting my baby. Being on our own creates space for silence and reflection. We've been whirling around in an other-worldly bubble and for the first time in what feels like a long time, this moment brings about a sharp sense of reality. Jamie was there for every second of a long labour, birth, and even throughout our overnight hospital stay. It feels like we've tackled the world together. We've shared the biggest moments of our lives with each other and his van leaving the drive feels like the end of an era. Back to normal. Yet, nothing about this is normal.

I'm excited to have my baby all to myself, whilst exploring the emotions, highs and lows of motherhood with no distractions. I'm not a teammate, a fiancée, or a daughter today. I'm a mum. The words feel strange yet exciting to type. I am a mum. I am a mum. I am a mum. *I am somebody's actual mum.* Yet, I'm apprehensive, because it feels like my body is in a state of shock. I worry about how it will hold up whilst simultaneously holding my baby. Ordinarily, I'd be on the sofa when I feel even a little bit like this. My brain is still foggy and my body still so beyond weary and sore from the C-section. The painkillers make me even more exhausted so I'm trying to get by on the lowest dose possible. *Does everyone take this long to heal?* There's no time to polish my broken jigsaw of feelings, though. Motherhood marches on.

My depleted body and mind have accepted that there's no time to rest, so we carry on carrying on, wondering what the implications will be. *How far can I push myself? At what point will my body give up from exhaustion? Will this bleeding ever stop?* I'm neglecting my needs so much that I'm worried I'll somehow break. "Pushing yourself" seems to be a theme that's synonymous with motherhood. It sometimes feels like my arms, legs and mind can't carry anymore, but being a new mum is one of the only jobs where taking a sick day isn't an option. We push through until it feels like we can't push anymore – then we're greeted by a new cry, full nappy, or hungry tummy (*again?*) and we somehow find an extra dose of energy to march on. Running on empty. Fuelled by love.

Though the gap between now and my last restful sleep is getting wider and solo parenting feels harder, motherhood seems to have become even more rewarding now that the newborn haze is lifting and we've become a mother-and-baby duo, flying solo. My motherly instincts seem to be guiding me through the parts that once felt tricky. Now, I feel our bond strengthening, as caring for him on my own makes me notice every detail even more. His silky skin seems even softer, his fluffy head smells even more powdery, his milky lips look even more tiny. His peachy body, plump tummy, and flailing limbs remind me of a salamander.

Salamander

It's week seven and you're smiling now
Then your tiny face scrunches
As you furrow your brow
You love to be nosy, so I carry you around
But still your bottom lip curls under
That was my warning
Now for the sound...

Your murmur gathers pace

It's sad to see discontent
Across your dear little face
As your baby lamb's cry gets bolder
I glimpse us in the mirror
Who's this nappy-clad salamander
Perched upon my shoulder?

Upon your dough body
Sits a little pea head
Dark almond eyes
Ultra long legs
Dimple for a chin
No neck yet
And arms?
You have chipolata sausages instead

You've frowned and you've screamed
Now let's get this crimson face
Back to a smiling sunbeam
I lower you onto the sofa
Noting how you're getting longer, growing taller
Then your long limbs cling around my arm
Like a branch hugged by a koala

Tapping your back as I drink cold tea
That's the moment you smile and gurgle at me
What are you saying? I'd love to know
I search your face for clues
Then your lips form that little "O"
Inquisitive yet wise as you scan the world
Long-blinking your eyes

These snapshots in time
I'll treasure forever
The season of no sleep
Emotional overload
No work, but working harder than ever

And every second of our time spent
Together.

WEEK 8

A rare diamond

My Incy Wincy Spider speeds down the spout with fireworks and fanfare, then WHOOSHES onto a slip and slide theme park.

Sometimes, you meet special people who bring warmth to a cold day and often without knowing, they place a reassuring hand on your shoulder when you're struggling. For me, that person is Ginny. She runs our local library's Baby Bounce group and, from the day I met her when I was seven months pregnant in the library, I knew she was one of those special people who everyone loves to be around. I discovered her group whilst reading a book about birth.

The quiet table I'd chosen for my research on the easiest way to get a baby from womb to world, was surrounded by prams, mums with muslin cloths slung over their shoulders, and most notably, a happy and carefree atmosphere. Even before my baby arrived, I felt excited by these momentary glimpses into the supportive motherhood community. I couldn't wait to officially be a member of the parenthood club. I could have navigated my way through the parked pushchairs and chosen a different table that day, but I didn't want to. I became entranced by the way Ginny engaged the babies and mums in her class. She remembered each of the little ones' names and made the newcomers feel at home. Her welcoming warmth was infectious and I enjoyed listening to the songs.

Around three months later, baby in my arms, I'm back at Ginny's class. I'm excited to introduce my little love to the world I've brought him into and am pleased that one of the first non-family members he meets is Ginny. She's the personification of calm, carefree happiness and clearly my son can sense it, too. He loves it here. I love it here. Everyone loves it here. Just like the happy vibes of home, I feel safe amidst the books, babies and other mums. I sense that Ginny has been through something in her life that fills her with caring superpowers; something that makes her stand out from the crowd. She's a rare diamond.

Editing this book from the future, I realise that in other, non-library groups, I'm singing songs with more gusto than everyone else. In other classes, once *Incy Wincy Spider* has climbed up the waterspout and the rain comes down, *Incy Wincy* washes down the pipe and falls to the floor. My *Incy Wincy Spider* speeds down the spout with fireworks and fanfare, then WHOOSHES onto a slip and slide theme park. At least, that's what it feels like when I realise I'm singing with Ginny's enthusiasm. Sometimes, I notice mums looking at me like I've taken something illegal. Nope, just high on Ginny's happy vibes.

Ginny

They don't come along often
They're always one of a kind
That certain special person
Who as soon as you meet them
They shine

I'm pregnant in the library
Flicking through books about birth
"How to stay calm and relax yourself
Then once your waters break
Here's what you need to do first..."

Across the room, I notice Ginny's baby class
Her smiley face
Calm
Enthusiasm
No book can teach you that

Her happy vibes warm the room
She's the sun peeking through on a cloudy day
I've never met this lady
But I can tell from those who surround her that
She certainly makes them feel that way

"Join us once your baby arrives?" she asks
When we chat
"We sing, talk, and play here every Thursday
And you can meet other mums

So please do come back"

So once my little one arrived
This is the first place we headed to
And of course
Ginny remembered us
Now we're official members of her happy crew

At-once elated, exhausted and struggling
But I'm in non-judgemental hands
Depleted body
Weary mind
Broken sentences
But Ginny understands

This class is our safe place
It makes these newborn days complete
Singing songs with other mums
Their babies
And Ginny

It's special seeing my baby grow here
Then I realise something about our magical friend
That once my boy's outgrown this class
Our short time of knowing Ginny
Will come to an end

We'll miss her calming influence
Her ability to sprinkle sunshine over everyone
But hopefully, I think to myself
She'll be here again
If we ever have another one?

WEEK 9

Finding a sisterhood in motherhood

No one ever speaks the words, but I think we all feel a sense of connection through this life-changing and wonderful, yet sometimes scary experience.

This week, I'm craving women. I'm still heterosexual, but after journeying through birth and new motherhood, there's something comforting about a certain kind of woman. I'm finding myself wanting to spend time with those who have done this before; those who have the same protective nature as me and understand what my body and brain have just been through – and what they're still going through. My detailed mind notes the magic, the strength, the softness of the women in my close-knit community of friends and family. Before me, stands a woman in a jumper, who happens to be my mum. Now that I'm a mum myself, I see an unsung superhero, wearing a soft cape and a light, floral fragrance that's ready to cocoon me in *Eau De Everything is Going to be Okay.*

I'm grateful for how the women in my life soften the sometimes-jagged edges of this experience. I appreciate the way my sister opens the door gently when she visits and how my friend Wendy speaks softly around us. No eye rolls, no judgement. Just pure support. Then there's the women I don't know very well but will always remember for their kindness during the lead-up to giving birth. There's one lady from my old workplace who plumped me with positivity before the big day and I still appreciate her for that. She didn't ask questions I didn't know the answer to, like if I was going to breastfeed (no idea. I'll try, but who knows if I'll be able to?) or what kind of birth plan I had (an elaborate one. She probably knew I may as well have sprayed it with perfume, decorated it with diamonds, then ripped it up and burnt it before we left for the hospital).

Instead, this lady who I had spoken to only a handful of times and was now messaging on Instagram, wrote of the beauty of motherhood. She wasn't overbearing or trying to throw scare stories or instructions into the mix. Instead, she detailed a few tips for what she found useful. This is where apps like Instagram shine. She finished her beautifully written monologue with: "Girl, there ain't no hood like motherhood". In hindsight,

I can now officially and wholeheartedly agree with her. This is quite the hood to be in.

I met another kind new mum in the library before the birth, who saw my bump and asked how I was feeling. I told her I was nervous. She asked which bit, specifically I was worried about. "Let's see if I can help", she said, before selflessly pulling up a seat and listening whilst I talked through how terrified I was at the thought of pushing a human head out of my… well, out of myself. My naive mind was picturing a watermelon, which couldn't have been any further from the reality. I'm sure this lady had enough to be getting on with as a new mum. She had another child at school and no doubt a house to tidy and food to eat. Maybe this was her moment of calm, where she could have had a shot at getting a warm cup of tea. Yet, she took the time to talk to me. She offered an understanding hand and provided a sense of balance amongst the conflicting thoughts, ideas and opinions. The kindness of a stranger.

This is when I realised that my impending motherhood had brought me into a sisterhood: a network of women who reach out to each other simply to chat, help, and provide support. No one ever speaks the words, but I think we all feel a sense of connection through this life-changing and wonderful, yet sometimes scary experience. I didn't know either of these women, yet our common ground of pregnancy and (my commencing) birth had led us to speak or write intimately, discussing in my case, the biggest unknowns of my life and tips for managing them. These ladies really did scoop me up and fill me with positivity, at a time when I really needed it.

Now whenever I find myself chatting to an expectant mum, I pay the kindness forward. I make the time to talk and ask how she's feeling. More often than not, we end up chatting about birth preferences, experiences and tips to help each other out. I feel there's something you go through, in becoming a mother, that brings you closer to other women who have been through the same. I'll forever be thankful to this period of my life for bringing me into this solid network of support – the sisterhood of motherhood.

The Best

This is the most sore
And bloated tummy

I think the world has ever seen
I haven't slept
I'm crying all the time
Yet, how am I?
I'm the best I've ever been

My partner's devoted arms
Now care for my baby son
I've never felt so
Vulnerable
Exposed
Second fiddle
Yet, it's the best thing I've ever done

My body's lost its shape for now
My head has turned to mush
These postnatal pains aren't my favourite
But
"How're you feeling?"
I'm overwhelmed with love

My days have lost routine
I'm routinely cleaning nappies and sick
Yet, amidst this newborn haze
No sleep
Losing myself
And tears of every kind
There's really no other way I'd have it

No one told me about the postpartum contractions
The leaking milk, or those six weeks of blood
Yet here I am still smiling because
As that kind mum once told me
There really is no hood
Like motherhood.

WEEK 10

Miracles, growth, and cheese on toast

For me, the excitement of watching him grow feels like the adulthood version of a school project, like when we used to grow cress out of a scooped-out eggshell filled with soil, so the cress looked like hair.

Isn't it interesting how the relationship between a parent or guardian and their child is one of the only relationships where one person stays largely the same, whilst the other continues to change each day? My baby knows me, but each time he wakes, I get to know a slightly different version of him. Every day, he grows a little taller, a little wiser, even cuter, and more charismatic. I'm fascinated. These changes will continue at a rapid rate, until he's a grown man. I don't know who that man is yet, but I'm enjoying the journey of finding out.

It almost feels too casual, that I'm sitting in my dressing gown eating cheese on toast whilst I watch this little miracle growing next to me. Shouldn't I be in a ball gown, celebrating with champagne or something? The cluster of cells I celebrated in my tummy is now here, living his sweet little life. Amidst the mundane moments of our daily routine, there's a small human who started off as stardust, and now that miracle is continuing his journey through the world so casually, as though this isn't an absolute miracle. His personality is in progress and his mannerisms are being made with each moment.

Though we all flex and morph like the changing scenes in a kaleidoscope throughout adulthood, it's gradual. By the time we're adults, we mostly know who we are and we build from there, slowly adding new hobbies and interests, dropping others, finding new facets of life that interest us along the way. It's fascinating to watch the process before that stage, of my son slowly morphing into a person I don't yet know. *What will his hobbies be? How will our relationship evolve?* Amidst the time I've spent labouring, loving, caring, sobbing and worrying, I note how beautifully he's growing and appreciate what a privilege this is.

For me, the excitement of watching him grow feels like the adulthood version of a school project, like when we used to grow cress out of a scooped-out eggshell filled with soil, so the cress looked like hair. I'd visit the kitchen windowsill each day to water my cress and check on its growth. Oh, the excitement, when its curly cress hair started to flop over the side of the shell. *Time for a haircut, my little egg man.* My eggshell baby was flourishing and I was its proud mum. I feel a similar excitement when my non-egg-based baby does something new – except now, the 365, 24/7 version of my cress head is all at once tiring and miles more rewarding, of course. Will I ever lose sight of how special this is? Never.

When You're a Grown Man

When you're a grown man
You won't remember any of this
The way you rooted for me with your eyes closed
I'm your strongest bond
Your most meaningful
Relationship

When you're a grown man
I'll be the same to you
You'll be a person I don't yet know
Though I'll be getting older
I'll still be the adult
Whose arms you were born into

I'll get to watch you grow
Come into your own
And all the while, my mind
Will hold this reflection of you
As my besotted child
My baby boy, now grown

You'll outgrow the body
Of my current best friend
Though some clues will still be there
Dad's dimple on your chin
The eyes you got from me
The swirl in the crown of your hair

When you're a grown man

Your face will have slenderized
Your gummy smile, replaced with teeth
I'll miss your koala-like button nose
And the way your profile is dominated
By those rounded little cheeks

Your smooth skin may be covered with stubble
Your wavering salamander arms will gain control
Your baby face will be replaced by photos
And memories that you'll never remember
But for me –
They're etched
Into
My
Soul.

WEEK 11

Simba's kingdom

It feels like I guided my Simba into the world with my right hand and showed him the planet he could have had, before taking it away with my left one.

Thinking of my boy as a grown man brings a lump to my throat for two reasons. First, it's the obvious thoughts of how I'll miss his baby face and the way my hand looks huge against his tiny bottom, which fits perfectly into my palm whilst I carry him to his bath. His diddy body won't always nestle into my lap as it does now, and the day will come when this delicate baby-bird-like boy no longer needs his head supporting or his body cradling. I'll never be conscious of the final time I cup him in my hands, as he'll gradually grow and morph into a man without me noticing. Then, one day, I'll need to hold him in the air, de-clasp my fingers, and watch him fly. He'll move from my protective shadow and branch out to create his own life. Though he'll forever be my number one, I understand I might not always be his. I'll be at peace with that, because my main priority is that my spirited seedling turns into a happy grown-up.

Then there's the second lump in my throat, which is brought about by pure guilt and a growing awareness of my own ignorance. As I introduce my baby to birds, buttercups, snow and sunshine, I feel like Mufasa, proudly presenting Simba with his kingdom. But something doesn't feel right. It feels like I guided my Simba into the world with my right hand and showed him the planet he could have had, before taking it away with my left one. I watch him looking around with carefree innocence whilst I'm riddled with eco-anxiety at the tangible reality of our climate crisis.

Look at the glaring audacity of me, introducing him to his planet, after playing a role in ruining it. Fast fashion. Disposable plastic. Throw-away goods. One day, our children will understand the part that we, as a generation, have played in damaging the earth through our single-use society. I recently heard a young child say that she doesn't want children of her own because she's worried that there won't be a world left for them to live in, after all the damage we've done to our planet. Those words from an innocent mouth felt painful to hear and I've never felt such guilt for partaking in that damage.

We've embraced the novelty of fast-moving technology, fast fashion and fast food, then taken it too far. Faster, longer, harder, more. There's a central theme of greed in modern times. We've loved technology and disposable items so much that we've squeezed them too hard. This advanced world is no longer a novelty. It's carcinogenic. What once was innovative and exciting, now often feels stressful and overwhelming. We sang the praises of our advancements, then prayed for the peace and simplicity of the days before this all existed.

This week, I take active steps to permanently slow our pace and embrace what the earth gave us. Editing this book from the future, growing ever-more conscious of our planet and how we spend our time here is the best move I could have made. Embracing a slower and simpler life has blessed me with wholesome times with my baby, that I otherwise never would have had. We pot plants in the garden, play in nature, and on rainy days, we bake, read, and build dens. Of course, we have days where we binge-watch cartoons or play with Playdough – that's balance. Our Mufasa and Simba days are the ones we enjoy the most though, so there's no need to get our dopamine hits from mass-buying toys and all sorts of disposable "stuff".

Our love for the simple life seems to be another part of parenthood that encourages negative attention. "He needs a toy kitchen at home", was a recent statement that seemed to warrant a response. Does he? I disagree. We play with toy kitchens and more at playgroups, so we have no reason to fill our home with this "stuff". He'd only get bored of it. "I heard you have a nice living room, but we thought it was going to be a playroom? Where are all the toys for your baby to play with?", remarked someone else. Cue: me lifting up the pouffe and opening the kitchen cupboards to reveal my organisational side. His favourite, most treasured toys nestle in boxes and even still, I think he has too many. That *"he should have more toys"* attitude has played a huge role in the breaking down of our planet and in my opinion, it's harmful to our children's maturing minds.

I loathe this continuing demand to justify myself to those who find it relevant to question the way we go about our parenthood. I also dislike the way excitement is often measured by material belongings. I make sure that with each gasp of "WOW! Look at this present – you lucky boy!" there's around three more excitable gasps of "EEK! How happy are we that your aunty has come to visit?!", "AWW, look at those lambs in the field", or "OOH I know, let's build a den and read our library books". My baby is never "denied" of over-stuffed cupboards of toys because I'm hell-bent on having a tidy home (though I do, admittedly, enjoy a tidy home); it's about teaching him to embrace the things that matter over actual "things". Amidst the thoughtless, material-minded comments, I'll continue to instil the value that our happiest days are made from memories, not plastic.

Going back to basics for a while feels liberating. As my WhatsApp messages and unread emails pile up, we read books in our favourite coffee shop and have picnics with our teddy bears in the park. The chaotic pace of the modern world is paused. Editing this from the future when my baby is almost eleven months old, gardening has become his favourite hobby. In fact, I'm realising that perhaps the old adage is true, that your baby grows up to like what you craved during pregnancy. With this boy's love for digging, mud, and smelling plants, I appear to have birthed a mini Alan Titchmarsh.

I'm Sorry for the Part I've Played

I'm sorry for the part I've played
In messing with the way our world is made

Blessed with golden sunsets and sparkling seas
Animals of all varieties

Tumbling waterfalls and starry nights
From colourful rainbows to the Northern Lights

We've enjoyed abundant beauty, then taken it for granted
Now I watch my baby play – knowing I've played a part in ruining his planet

We shake our heads at global warming
Then shrug our shoulders at every warning

I pour milk from disposal plastic
Then throw another landfill item into the skip

I sob over a skinny polar bear who's lost his food and home
Before filling my basket with fast-fashion clothes

Eyes glazed; hearts made of guilt
We're spoiling their futures with this disposable world we've built

Why are big companies making this so hard for us?
What was wrong with glass milk bottles and non-disposable goods?

This needs to stop before the world does
What's harming them is caused by us

I've ignorantly watched the world waste away
Then exclaimed: "How strange! Sunburn and frostbite on the same day?"

I'm Mufasa, presenting Simba with his kingdom
Except I gave it with my right hand, took it with my left one

I'm so sorry for the part I've played
In messing with the way our world is made

There were unspoiled landscapes and clear blue seas
But disposable goods, ignorance and greed

They came
In too many varieties.

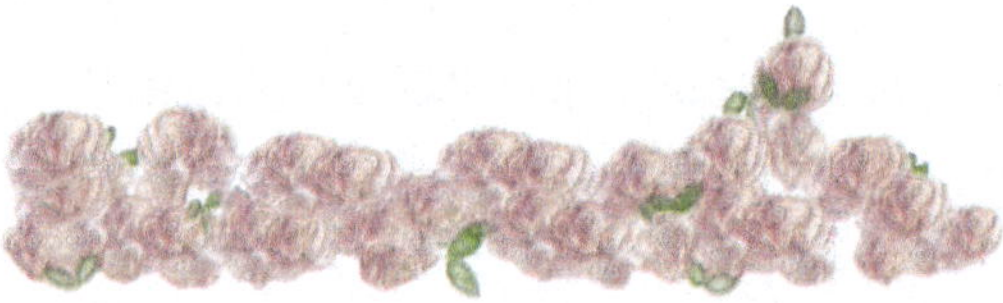

WEEK 12

That's what makes a mum like this

Amidst the rubble, I've found a treasure trove of superpowers that make me proud to have a mind like mine and thankful to be a mum like this.

This week's entry is going to be a tricky one to write. I'd like to highlight the struggles and superpowers I've been living with since I was in my early teens, which have brought me to where I am today. This chapter details the condition that's led me to press the self-destruct button on many aspects of my life and watch it crumble to pieces around me. It's about what's knocked me over, built me up, re-arranged my entire life, and resulted in the pride, empathy, creativity and determination that comes with being a mum like this. Trigger warning: this chapter contains a brief mention of thoughts about death. For those with sensitive hearts like mine, breastfeeding mums looking to keep those oxytocin levels high, or for those who simply don't want to read about this topic, please skim over the eighth and ninth paragraph down from this one.

I was in my early teens when I began to spend a fortnight or more unpicking perhaps the *healthiest* parts of my life, throwing them up in the air and watching as they burned to the ground. In that timeframe, I'd feel heartbroken and depleted, even when nothing notable had happened. A steady, dull ache bled through my muscles into the very tips of my fingers and toes. Talking, walking, thinking and moving all became a struggle. My chest area was so sore that it hurt to move my arms or hug anyone. An X-ray concluded that my boobs were, as the nurse worded it, "absolutely full of cysts", which explained why I couldn't lift my arms above waist height and needed to sleep in a den of perfectly-placed pillows. My reflections in windows highlighted why my family kept checking in often: I could hide my upset heart but pure distress was prominently sewn into the fabric of my face.

One day, I'd be the most confident person in the room; the next I'd want to be alone for a couple of weeks. I'd spend hours or days in the most isolated pits of my body and mind, staring into space, unable to break out of the lonely haze and immerse myself back into the reality I was so homesick for. I'd watch an entire film and not take any of it in. I'd have conversations with friends and family, then later wonder what the conversation was about and whether they noticed that my soul seemed to have left my body. It felt like a monster had taken over my mind and had a hold of my wrists and neck, as it snatched me away from the people I love.

Holding down friendships and relationships felt impossible with this condition. Relationships would be intense or not at all. I'd be happy with a boyfriend, but a need to be alone took over, so I'd call it off suddenly and without warning, then the cycle would begin again. This led to my surname – Taylor – being affectionately adapted by my friends into my nickname: Taylor Swift. Swift's songs felt like they were written for me and they've helped me through every breakup. We all made a joke of the similarities between mine and her conveyor belt of relationships. Looking back though, my behaviour was rooted in a really dark place.

Similarly, when it came to friendships, I was the absolute *Casper* of ghosting people, as a coping mechanism for craving so much time alone. Other than my three closest friends, I used to turn my back on friendships with the same force as I did with relationships. Not because I didn't respect those people; not because I didn't value those friendships. It was because I knew that those people deserved more than I could give them when I felt detached from myself and from the world.

I often had an impaired view of my identity, regularly reinventing myself, my clothes and my home. Once, I broke up with a boyfriend and by the time he came to pick up his clothes, he remarked: "You've re-designed your whole home. It looks completely different?" I laughed it off with an "oh, you know me! What am I like!" Really, I knew that reinventions had become an important part of an identity that I could never quite pin down. I spent a lot of time feeling as though I was living in a parallel universe to everyone else – until the fourth week of my menstrual cycle.

In that fourth week, I'd spring back to life, brimming with ideas, creativity, and excitement, as though nothing had ever happened. I'd act as though I hadn't just driven a digger through a healthy relationship, cut off all my friends, done a U-turn on my hobbies, torn down my interiors, hibernated from my family and generally set fire to everything that was going well in my life. I swept all those ashes under the rug and embraced the high life for the week that it lasted, before inevitably tearing it all down again. I was confused as to how my life had taken on such a staccato rhythm as my mood seemed to keep jolting in opposite directions – but I was just happy to experience the ecstasy of that fourth week, before the monster returned. It felt like the low times were so bad, that I unlocked a new level of happiness in that fully content week. I seemed to have been blessed with superpowers which, beyond the disorder, made me capable of feeling ecstatic highs and achieving life and career milestones that I perhaps wouldn't have otherwise. I never took that happiness for granted or let that magical week go to waste, so I pushed myself hard to progress in my work and personal life during that short timeframe.

The only lasting product of this constructive week though, was my career. Beneath the black clouds and brain fog, my writing has remained the only constant that I could pour my heart into and continue to progress with. I believe the introverted nature of my profession is what has turned my career into a steady tonic that's helped me through everything during my teenage and adult life; everything else fell to pieces again, following that one wonderful week. I'd phase-out the friends I'd made, cut off whichever relationship I'd been nurturing and feel myself slowly zoning back out of the world that I so desperately wanted to belong in.

Amidst the physical and emotional ruin, I'd see a flurry of family and friends reaching out their kind hands and comfort blankets, but it felt like they were behind a window, in a world I wasn't part of. I could hear their muffled voices and see them scrambling to help, but I could never quite reach them. The monster was sweeping me away and making me too unwell to tell anyone about whatever this scary darkness was that was storming through my body and mind. So, I'd spend my loneliest hours thinking about how I could take myself onto an empty road in the middle of the night and drive at full speed into the central reservation to make everything stop.

I dreamed of the airbag cuddling my body tightly and safely, whilst my soul flew up to the sky, to look down on life from above. Worryingly, these didn't feel like sad or harmful thoughts, at the time. I still wanted to exist, just without the exhaustion that came with every aching muscle and without the thoughtful mind and sensitive heart, which made life feel so difficult. I craved an existence where I wasn't required to hold down friendships or relationships or to live with a body that felt like it didn't work. This segment of my life feels scary when I think back on it with a much clearer mind, but at the time, ending my life seemed like an exciting chance for liberation.

Then came pregnancy and just like that, all the symptoms evaporated. It felt like somebody had focussed my lenses and for the first time in my adult life, I could see straight. Despite having my head down the toilet with 24/7 pregnancy sickness, the thunder turned to sunshine, the ravaging waves turned into a peaceful lake and the bitter taste of life turned to sweet freedom. In fact, it felt like everything I'd ever known had been turned the right way around. I was the happiest, most carefree I'd ever been and couldn't believe that this was how simple and enjoyable life could be for *the full four weeks* of a month. I'd never felt this steady level of happiness before. Whilst I heard others complaining of the discomfort of pregnancy, I was like a kid in a sweet shop – with extra lollies and a cherry on top. And sherbet. Plus a flake.

I was tired, sick and also flourishing on a whole new level. Never, have I ever, thrived so much as I did throughout pregnancy. It was a refreshingly wonderful sense of what others must experience as "normal". Each day felt like a relief, to wake up feeling a steady sense of joy. The monster had gone and I was optimistic that he wouldn't return. I'd read that throughout pregnancy, certain aspects of our bodies and emotions or things we struggled with before, sometimes never go back to exactly how they once were. Whether that's adult acne, dry hair or in my case, tricky emotions, my positive mind was sure that I'd exited that rollercoaster for good. Pure relief. These new, steadily happy emotions had me feeling like Ariel from *The Little Mermaid* when she saw her new legs for the first time and brushed her hair with a fork. This world felt untouched. I'd never seen my adult life through these eyes before. Everything was shiny, exciting and new to me. No more going mind-blind. No more aching body. No more all-consuming suicidal thoughts. Just a life full of happiness, thriving friendships and a steady sense of identity. I wanted to forever be part of this world.

Then the monster returned. It happened recently over a couple of days. My body and mind seemed to morph from my new-found self, back into the restricted version of me. It was like the transformation scene from *Cinderella* when she leaves the palace in her ball gown with a perfectly polished bun, and by the time she reaches home, she's shoeless and her posh dress is replaced with rags. My monster announced its return with unexplained vomiting over a couple of nights and boobs full of cysts. Once again, my chest area became so painful that I could hardly move or hug anyone. I woke up unable to lift my arms, as the physical symptoms swept back through my body. My temporarily lustrous skin reverted to the painfully dry version that I'm used to, whilst fatigue and brain fog bulldozed their way back into my life and aching muscles made it too exhausting to move. Then came the grand finale: my steady mood was replaced with that rollercoaster of emotions I knew so well.

I'd glimpsed life through steadily happy lenses and now the monster was back, postpartum, with a vengeance. After seeing how life could be beyond this condition, this was when I *knew* I needed to seek help. Clearly, this had to be a cyclical issue. I'd been suffering with these symptoms for 21 years, and it couldn't have been a coincidence that they went away during pregnancy. I'd also previously been diagnosed with a meningioma; a benign brain tumour, which the neurosurgeon explained can be influenced by female hormones. This experience was *surely* hormonal and it was time to listen to my family who had, for a number of years, encouraged me to see a specialist. I visited a consultant gynaecologist and within the hour, my struggles had an explanation and my condition had a name: Premenstrual Dysphoric Disorder (PMDD).

To summarise it in a sentence, PMDD is a "serious disorder that can negatively affect your life, relationships and career".[4] For an issue that I've forever felt alone with, my diagnosis led me to discover a wide and far-reaching community of "alone" women, just like me. One story has particularly embedded itself into my memory. I heard it from a fellow PMDD-sufferer of child-bearing age. This lady was desperate to have children, but her PMDD was ruining her life to the extent that she saw no option but to have a hysterectomy. Post-recovery, she feels great – other than the baby-shaped hole in her heart that PMDD stole from her.

PMDD is often referred to as – even sometimes masked as – Premenstrual Syndrome (PMS), but for the women who suffer, that conclusion is far from accurate. The descriptions of this condition never quite capture the dangerously debilitating, life-altering impacts of it. In fact, before my diagnosis, doctors insisted for years that I was suffering from a simple case of PMS with depression and needed to "take painkillers and get on with it, because that's life for many women, unfortunately". So, they'd slide another Sertraline prescription across the table, beam me a smile, and I'd be on my way, dreading the next time that monster returned and I had no strength to push him off.

Eventually, I stopped visiting my GP because their pop a pill and chill method wasn't working. Paracetamol didn't take away the dark thoughts, hormone-related brain tumour or cystic boobs. I couldn't hug a hot water bottle to stop me from ending yet another perfectly fine relationship or turning my back on friendships. The highest dose of Sertraline didn't stop me from not wanting to see anyone, including my closest friends and family for days, sometimes weeks – nor did it answer any of the questions as to why my brain wouldn't function and why I felt so desperately low. For me, this highlights a flaw in the diagnosis of PMDD.

I was treated for depression for 21 years. When I finally sought specialist help and highlighted to the consultant gynaecologist that the highest dose of Sertraline wasn't working, she stated that it was never going to. "You've never had depression", she said, "this is a hormone imbalance, so Sertraline may have taken the edge off the associated anxiety, but we need to focus on balancing your hormones". *21 years later and I've never had depression?* How was this missed, for so long, when I was presenting all the classic symptoms of a hormone imbalance? Alongside the psychological impacts, my PMDD presented itself physically. I was told by a specialist that my meningioma was likely caused by a hormonal imbalance. I was told that my breasts were filled with cysts, because of hormones. I was told that my inability to move freely on the days when my body ached, was likely down to a hormone imbalance. I'd presented all these symptoms – physical and psychological – clearly in diary form and begged for a diagnosis but still, I was told I had a simple case of depression with bouts of PMS.

It wasn't the fault of the GPs. At the time of writing this book, they're not currently trained to recognise the symptoms of PMDD, though I believe there are talks being held by the UK Parliament with a view to changing this. If I hadn't explored the private healthcare route, my PMDD never would have come to light. A diagnosis of such a life-altering issue should not be reserved for those who can afford to pay – or be paid for. Many women with this disorder are being let-down. Women with any form of hormonal issue are being let down on a daily basis as society rolls its eyes, whispers "women issues" and awkwardly turns away.

After reflecting on how much this condition has affected my life and chatting with other women who have had far worse PMDD-related experiences than mine, I'm concerned for fellow sufferers who haven't been diagnosed – those who maybe never will be. There are women living with this condition who haven't been able to see beyond the PMDD haze, so have taken their own lives, had their wombs removed, or lived their entire menstruating lives behind the window that I was stuck behind for so long. The root cause needs to be found and treated in these cases, before any more women turn to drastic measures. I can see all too easily how some feel compelled to make irreversible decisions based upon how impossible PMDD is to escape from. If you don't know you have it, how can you be equipped to deal with it? Paracetamol can't stop hormones from running wild, nor can a meditation podcast fix suicidal thoughts when they're puppeteered by hormones. These women need a peaceful diagnosis and specialist help.

Though I'm at the beginning of my treatment journey, I see now, through my enlightened eyes, how I found it hard to simply live – let alone hold down a normal life, relationship and friendships with this condition. There was no way I could fit an entire life, relationship, career and friendship circle into that one, steady week; not when my life was like a scene from *Mrs Doubtfire*. Just like Robin Williams' character Daniel, I was flitting between two starkly different personas. I was trying to act "normal" whilst attempting to soothe my PMDD-flawed self behind the scenes. Just like Daniel in that famous *Mrs Doubtfire* cake-face scene, when I came up against a plan from a friend, I'd need to dip my face into a metaphorical cream cake, mask my puffy eyes and pre-plan conversations to make socialising easier on my foggy mind. Once all that was done, it was a simple case of "coming right up, dear!" Getting to that stage though, was exhausting in itself.

Even if I could have squished friendships into a one-week timeframe, I'd have had no time for anything else. That week was dedicated to recovering from the exhaustion of the previous weeks and doing everything on fast-forward – a desperate attempt to live a normal life and tick off all the goals that the high-achieving version of me dreamed of, beyond my PMDD.

Along with the symptoms that I now know to be PMDD, I've always had an awareness of how my brain works slightly differently to what may be described as "neurotypical". So, to cover all bases on my journey to figuring myself out, I had an appointment with a consultant psychologist from The Priory, where it became evident that I'd been living with a mild neurodivergent "disorder". Everyone with this form of condition is different, but for me, it's characterised by sensory overwhelm (particularly with bright lights and noise), an acute awareness of emotions (both the good and bad), needing to spend a lot of time alone / pushing people away and long-term feelings of emptiness and loneliness. Of course, PMDD and a neurological "disorder" don't complement each other.

Since researching and learning ways to soothe the lows and harness the magic that lives alongside the highs, I've unearthed something special. Amidst the rubble, I've found a treasure trove of superpowers that make me proud to have a mind like mine and thankful to be a mum like this. This journey is tough, without a doubt. Now that I can see clearer though, I've found that beneath the dark clouds, these conditions have blessed my already-detailed thoughts with extra empathy, creativity, calm and determination. I see magic in the mundane. In black-and-white scenes, I see swathes of colour and detail. My little bubble of life is usually calm and happy, as I embrace every good day and each pocket of calm whilst it exists. I have a strong sense of self-awareness, with intense empathy for others. My neurodivergent mind strengthens the bond I share with my baby, too. I'm particularly sensitive to his needs and tuned-in to his emotions. From the games, stories and songs I create, to the dens I build and dances I choreograph in our kitchen to make him laugh – I'm not sure any of this would be up to its high creative standard, without my thoughtful mind and sensitive heart.

Of course, even on the road to recovery, life isn't always sunshine and lollipops. As I now proudly live with these two conditions that often clash with each other, the sunshine and lollipops often turn to thunderstorms and vomit fruit. The difference now though, is that I've made friends with the thunder and my taste buds have grown to tolerate the bad flavour brought about by the sad times. Nowadays, whilst the intense highs are still naturally interwoven with crashing lows, I've learned to find comfort in discomfort. I embrace the positive symptoms and nurture the negative ones, and this has led my neurodivergent mind to thrive. I've learned that, even aside from PMDD, sad times are just as normal as the happy times and they're more comfortable when I ride – rather than resist – the waves. Despite the Disney films, fairy tales and social media stories we're conditioned to compare our lives to, I've discovered that feeling bad isn't *bad.* Once I've made it to a safe island in my mind, where I can manage sadness, I've witnessed those "bad' feelings living together with feeling on top of the world. Feeling "bad" is my clever little signal that tells me to stop, look after myself and recharge my superpowers, ready for another round of seeing life through my fascinating, kaleidoscopic lenses. For me, feeling "bad" is simply a by-product of being able to harness the creativity, determination, empathy, and ambitious drive that thrive alongside my PMDD.

I see similar qualities in others with neurodivergent minds. My son and I often visit The Ark Café in Northwich. It's run by a charity called "ChAPS", which supports autistic people across Cheshire. Many autistic people work and gather at the café and I see their superpowers shining through each time we visit. Outside of this café, there's a world filled with small talk, "I don't mind"s, and awkward chats about the weather. Here, the conversations have depth; they have meaning. I've joined in with fascinating conversations about everything from dreams for the future, self-soothing methods for the tricky days, cleaning, cakes and crafts. The café team and their friends and supporters take life and add sparkles to it. They create garden-scapes that welcome you in. They make crafts that they sell in their shop, and for special occasions, they decorate the humble café with bunting and banners. Here stands another inclusive community which, just like the library, radiates a special sense of support and comfort. The people here have an awareness and appreciation of personal space. You can go in for a chat or sit alone to recharge and nobody cares – in a good way. Everybody here seems fuss-free, creative and calming. They have mannerisms that I enjoy being around, but don't tend to see often in the "outside world". Neurodivergent minds are magical.

On the topic of magic, I can't talk about being a mum like this without mentioning my fiancé *and* fellow sufferer of an endocrine condition, Jamie.

When we first met, I hadn't realised that kissing those frogs had led me, "Taylor Swift", to meet my match. Of course, I hadn't yet been diagnosed with PMDD, so when the inevitable moment came in the early days of dating – when I needed to retreat into myself, end the relationship, and set about the reinvention process once again – Jamie became the first man in my life to extend an understanding hand. I was shocked into the alarming realisation that he seemed to know the inner workings of my mind, without fully knowing me. It turned out that he had suffered with similar struggles. Whilst his condition is related to blood sugar, rather than hormones, Jamie told me he'd spent years feeling cut-off, drifting from one day to the next, not remembering much, and not feeling much passion towards anything or anyone. What are the chances that, out of everyone in the world, his hand would find mine and we'd be able to hold each other's through the stormy times? In fact, Jamie is the first man I've met who's understood the brain fog and the craving for solitude. At my lowest, when I was unable to put all the tricky feelings into words, he verbalised them for me. For the parts that even he couldn't understand, we'd unscramble them together.

I never dreamed of finding a man who would even try to understand this condition – let alone help me to build a nest whenever the PMDD monster has reared his head. Yet here we have a man who just "gets it". Wherever possible, he's given me the space and grace to simply ride the emotional wave. Jamie stuck by me through that tempestuous yet pivotal year and encouraged me – alongside my other close family members – to seek the diagnosis that changed my life. He's witnessed the superpowers that lie behind a mind like mine and a mum like this. He's my boldest supporter through everything from my career and being a modern mum, to writing this book, always embracing and championing the way my mind and body works.

Likewise, I see the treasure that lies in his mind. Since learning to manage his blood sugar struggles, his self-proclaimed "dull and grey brain" has come alive with colour, texture and emotion. He's still as practical-minded as ever – still the black and white to my colour and the straight-talking side to my dreamy personality. Yet, he often says he's thankful for his endocrine condition, because now that he's learned to control the blood sugar and brain fog, he's unlocked a new level of happiness, healthiness and emotion that he's never experienced before. He knows what it feels like to be paralysed by his own mind, so now that he's broken out of it, he embraces every waking moment. He celebrates the beauty of life without the mind-blindness and the physical impacts of that. We both do.

Jamie and I agree that, now we've found ways to soothe our conditions, the discomfort of our past experiences has turned to rocket fuel and on our good days, we're more determined than ever to harness our superpowers. We know how limiting life can feel beneath the surface of those good days. I'm grateful for the extra superpowers that lie in not just one, but *two* "different" minds – particularly when it comes to nurturing and understanding our son. Amidst the pressures of the modern world which seem to dictate that everyone should be happy, fulfilled and thriving in life 100% of the time, Jamie and I will remind our child that hard times make the good times flourish.

We'll raise our boy to appreciate that differences aren't deficits, that it's normal for bad days to live alongside the good, and that sadness often comes with superpowers. We hope he'll enjoy the freedom that comes with the knowledge that – whether you're the happiest person in the world or your emotions get knocked over sometimes – it is possible to find comfort in gloomy times and, in fact, once you've made it to a safe island where you can see straight, those feelings can be turned into treasure. So yes, if I had to swap my hormone imbalance and personality "disorder" for another one, I'd 100% choose to keep myself the way I am. Though I'm still trialling different treatments for PMDD, since identifying my condition and in turn, discovering a toolkit of tricks that help me to soothe it, I'm proud to be the reactive and attentive mum that I am. I'm proud of what makes a mind like mine. I'm proud to be a mum like this.

A Mum Like This

Kaleidoscopic mind
Imprisoned in a painful body
Hurtling through sunshine and thunderstorms
The contradictions of PMDD

I feel everything like I'm an exposed nerve
Emotions appear in **bold**, underlined, with *emphasis*
I find sadness and joy in the tiniest things

I’ve met the lowest lows and sweetest bliss

Here it is – it’s returned
I’m wrestling with this ever-changing brain
Two weeks going steady and then –
Oh, look
I've ghosted everyone again

Because at the core of the sad times
Lies this desperation to turn everything off
My phone, my friends, my thoughts
I
Need
To
Just
Stop

These bricks fall down so suddenly
That’s how I start ghosting everyone
Relationships will be going great
Until the devil comes back
I close the book
And consider that chapter done

I’ve definitely loved and lost
Pushed countless friends away
Friends who I truly valued
But the confusion and exhaustion and
The need to be alone got in the way

Because the simplest thing becomes a trigger
The tiniest detail knocks my insides out like dominoes
I feel pain from the top of my foggy head
To the tips of my fragile glass toes

A symptom that’s rarely spoken about
It’s discussed less than PMDD itself:

How a mind like this thrives with detail and empathy
Imbued with creativity and determination
Through every sensitive cell

I'm grateful for my diagnosis
For clearing the fog from my eyes
So I could work to overcome the worst bits
And wear the best bits
With pride

I don't drift through life
Taking everything for granted
I work hard, I appreciate things
The few friendships I have are deep
And meaningful
And candid

Everything I do
Any project I focus on
Once I've shed blood
And sweat
And tears
That's when I know I'm done

They say it's a blessing and a curse
To know crashing lows
Alongside pure, ecstatic bliss
On the good days
I realise how lucky I am
To have a mind like this

I'm the attentive mum to my son I hoped I'd be
I'm protective over my time – and his
I'm filled with creativity and empathy
That's what makes a mind like mine
That's what makes a mum like this.

WEEK 13

Nursery rhymes and new friends

You're likely to meet some love-forever friends who at some point, you won't be able to imagine life without.

As mentioned last week, I find it overwhelming to have lots of friends. I believe it's linked with the need to often reinvent myself, as well as the exhaustion that sometimes comes with having a mind like mine. How can I expect people to accept me for who I am, when even I'm not sure who I will be on that day? I could be the me who's creative, chatty, ready to have a million deep conversations about everything. Or I could be the person who can't talk to anyone; who can't turn the TV or radio on. I've grown to love both iterations of myself, yet I understand that my hot-then-cold approach doesn't make for great friendships.

The few friends I've had since childhood have strong roots, ingrained deep within rich soil. These friends know me inside out. They know my need for alone time and my preference for a diary that remains empty for spur-of-the-moment plans. We're a permanent fixture within each other's lives, yet because we don't see each other often, I'm never embroiled in dramas, or anything that goes awry with "normal" friendships. My small handful of friends often confide in me with problems and worries, because my thoughtful mind and sensitive heart bless me with many of the hallmark qualities of a faithful friend. I'm empathetic and caring. My detailed, analytical thinking can sort other people's problems out, fast. They can count on me never being tempted to talk bad about them to my non-existent group of friends – as so often seems to be the case in large circles.

I miss the post-teenagehood friends I've made and then inevitably broken away from as an adult. I miss Rachel and I miss Catherine and I miss all the other friendships that my PMDD ran away with. But how does an adult explain these unique personality traits to another adult? That's something I've struggled with and eventually turned a blind eye to. How do I apologise for the fact that I'm riddled with social anxiety over our next wonderful plan? How do I explain to potential friends that it's perhaps best to avoid me because eventually I'll ghost them anyway? My loved-and-lost friends all deserved a consistency that I've never felt capable of beyond my immediate, small friendship group.

Yet, as I continue to grow and learn all sorts of wonderful and uncomfortable truths about myself throughout motherhood, I've finally found a comfortable balance when it comes to maintaining friendships. I've discovered that parenthood friends don't come with the pressure I used to run away from. The structure of meeting as-and-when at baby groups provides a natural springboard for carving beautiful relationships with fellow mums. We attend classes with our babies together and occasionally meet up outside of those groups. I feel a strong connection with these people, through seeing them on a weekly basis and being on the emotional rollercoaster of raising humans together. It may sound silly, but for the first time in my life, I've learned how to cultivate and embrace the beauty of having friends – and keeping them. I love it and wish I'd learned all of this sooner.

Even in my short thirteen weeks of parenthood so far, these ladies have become an anchor in the haze when I've felt overwhelmed by the tricky days that we all encounter every now and then. We've seen each other on the good days, as well as in those moments when you've not slept, your bones ache and you've got toothpaste down your top. We've been there to witness each other's balance and I never feel pressure or judgement. This must be what I've been missing out on with friendships for such a long time. Once again, I feel like an alien that's figuring the world out for the first time as an adult.

Forming friendships with these mums reminds me of when you go to school and, though you don't get to pick who's in your year or class, you'll undoubtedly share everyday experiences with some of the people you're grouped together with, which strengthens your familiar bond. You're likely to meet some love-forever friends who at some point, you won't be able to imagine life without. No matter what year you were in, you'll probably argue forever that yours was the best. That's how I feel. This mum-class of mine is the crème de la crème of mum friends, in my opinion.

I met most of my new friends at Baby Bounce and Rhyme Time, when I didn't know any of their names, but I always felt happy to see the friendly faces of Ted's mum, Ru's mum, Olive-Grace's mum, George's mum, Albie's mum and Zac's mum. I feel a particular affinity with Zac's mum, whose name I now know to be Kerys. She seems to understand my love for lots of time alone or with my family in favour of a calendar filled with plans and large mum-group meetups. I find that with each sentence I begin, Kerys can finish it for me, whilst accurately capturing how I feel. She also appears to crave the same kind of calm as I do. No stress, no pressure to meet up regularly and fill the calendar with plans – just pleasant, pressure-free company that enriches my motherhood experience. I hope that my company enhances her journey through parenthood, too.

The library, where we come to Baby Bounce, is my calm and happy place – the perfect, stress-free backdrop for kindling new friendships. The smell of the books, the tippy-tappy of the librarians on the computer, the sense of calm when you walk by the person who has sat down to read a book quietly in the corner. It reminds me of how my favourite film character feels about her trips to her favourite place. In *Breakfast at Tiffany's*, Holly Golightly says that Tiffany's calms her down "right away". "The quietness and the proud look of it; nothing very bad could happen to you there", she says. That's how I feel, sitting amongst the brightly-coloured books of Northwich library, with the tired-faced, lovely mums and the sense of nostalgia brought about by nursery rhymes.

Some would no doubt find it boring that after a few years of holidays, nights out, and extended adventures to Australia, I'm actually enjoying being back in my hometown the most; soaking in the experiences of the simple life through my parental eyes. There was a time when I preferred travelling and partying over anything. Through this season of my life, I'm not craving a holiday or a cocktail. I find joy in discovering the beauty of motherhood.

Baby Bounce

Here we are at Baby Bounce
Shy faces looking around
We're only singing nursery rhymes
Yet this all feels profound

I'm fascinated, seeing you in the wide world
Your dimpled hand clasping mine
I grew your heartbeat in my tummy

Now we're bouncing to the beats
Of nostalgic nursery rhymes

Old MacDonald had a farm E-I-E-I-Oh my!
I study each intricately detailed ear
Chubby thighs
These ten tiny toes
Expressive eyes

My body didn't need to think about what it was doing
Though I was sick through the night, noon and morning
All because inside me, you were growing
And this is why I get emotional when we sing...

You are my sunshine, my only sunshine
You make me happy when skies are grey
My son shines
New meaning on my life
In the most
Wonderful way

We fan the sparkle-spangled net
Above your friends and yourself
How have I found purpose
Singing about Incy Wincy Spider
The prickly hedgehog
And everybody else?

It's because I grew your head
Shoulders
Knees and toes
Knees and toes
And eyes and ears and mouth and nose
Used to wonder who my baby would be
Now I'm watching you grow

I've experienced motherhood's ecstatic highs and plunging lows

I'm in the same boat as everyone in this room
We all feel the choppy water
And know the waves will calm again soon

So we row, row, row our boats
Gently down the stream
I have my baby
Cruising along with me
Is this real or is this a dream?

Spent nine months wondering
"Who will this miracle be?"
Now that magic and stardust
Is laying right here in front of me

Twinkle, twinkle little star
Oh, how I used to wonder
But now I'm discovering
Exactly
Who you are.

WEEK 14

(Anti)social media

Online networking was no longer a novelty for me, but the refreshing reality of ignoring it was.

Amidst the new friends, nursery rhymes and personal growth, I realise I've been blissfully neglecting something that once drained a large amount of my time: social media. For me, the term "antisocial media" seems more fitting. Thinking back to pre-motherhood, I used to hold my phone more than my favourite writing pen, my fiancé's hand, or whichever novel I could barely put down. I'd grasp my phone more than hot chocolates and cosy blankets in the winter and more than picnic baskets and ice creams in the summer. In hindsight, I wince at the time I wasted scrolling around a screen in favour of doing wholesome things that made my heart happy. Since my son arrived, I've spent more time holding him than my phone. It feels liberating and I wish I'd tried this sooner. Although, it seems that in the modern world, this is an unpopular way to be.

Sometimes, friends and acquaintances talk about their lives as though I've been living alongside them. Confused faces stare back at me when I ask them questions that I'd have known the answers to, had I been living in their pockets. It seems I've let them down by not keeping up on social media. I find it tricky to keep up with the fast pace of the modern world itself; letting that flood through to my phone would definitely feel overwhelming. Plus, why would I pay a phone bill each month for something that stresses me out? That's insanity.

Social media often doesn't seem very sociable, to me. The modern world seems so brainwashed by the networking apps that it's easy to miss the irony. Instagram tricks us into thinking we're socialising, whilst stealing our *actual* social time from behind our backs when we're too busy scrolling to notice. It's clever, really. Sharing and seeing others' life updates is exciting to begin with, so the novelty is addictive. Before long, you realise that if you don't post anything interesting for a while, it seems to the online world that you haven't *done* anything interesting for a while; or worse, you develop a fear of missing out on big announcements and exciting news because we've all become so dedicated to the app. That's how we get sucked into the antisocial, "social" media cycle.

Since becoming conscious of social media's ability to drain my time, WhatsApp, text messages, Instagram and Facebook have all been muted on my phone. Why was I letting those apps control me? Now, I only see messages and updates when I mindfully log onto those platforms. My loved ones understand the sense of order, peace and calm that this brings to my life – and they tend to do the same. It's a shared value that we've each nurtured and felt the freedom of. We know we can ring each other when needed and we no longer feel the overwhelming demands of our devices. Phone freedom is underrated.

During a recent visit to York Minster, I noticed the extent to which people are controlled by their devices. As I noted the wonder on my baby's face at the grandeur of the cathedral, I found myself mesmerised by the scenes playing out behind him. Before us, stood a 7th-century architectural masterpiece bustling with tourists, yet not one single person was admiring its beauty through their own eyes. *Not one single person.* Everyone was staring blankly into their phone cameras and moving from one room to another, without taking their eyes away from the scenes being captured by their devices. Each phone-faced tourist bustled past the next, clamouring to capture the best images and live streams. They'd have been better off tapping "York Minster" into YouTube and saving the travel cost. Nothing about their actions looked mindful. They seemed like zombies, controlled by machines.

To me, the way social media is taken so seriously and plays such an integral part in modern society is scary. It reminds me of the kind of warped world you'd see on *Black Mirror*. If I can't go back to the good old days of uploading – and then forgetting about – a picture of my cocktail to Instagram with nothing accompanying it but the vignette filter and one "like" (from my ever-supportive mum), do I want to go back at all? I'm not sure I do. Recently, I've noticed that a genuine and widespread concern has emerged amidst the Instagram users I follow: "Please show my post some love – people aren't seeing me". I forever support small businesses, but why are individuals who don't have Instagram as an income stream, upset about not being "visible" on an app? Surely, it's better to be visible in the real world? Surely these people should know how wonderfully worthy they are, beyond the "likes" that do or don't roll in on an app?

Writers publish articles, essays and books about the innovative, healing art of putting down your phone and "logging off". What a novelty! What a treat! I'd originally stepped back from the social media circus for one month, but that month turned into a year. Online networking was no longer a novelty for me, but the refreshing reality of ignoring it was. I enjoyed not silently judging the people posing with balloons to celebrate how many followers they had on an app, or those apologising for not being present on their stories since yesterday. I'll never let my mind be clouded and muddled by the smoky veil of social-media-staging again. Instead, I revel in the bliss of not knowing what every Tom, Dick and Harry had for their breakfast, lunch and tea. I'll be over here, living a calm and wholesome life. Most of all, I'll be holding my baby's hand more than my phone.

Promise to My Baby

You'll only be a baby for a short while
It's my time to show you the world I've brought you into
So as you sleep by my side
Here's my promise to you

I promise I'll be emotionally present
I won't spend our time scrolling Instagram
Hoping that if I post endless staged photos
People might think I'm the kind of mum I already know I am

I promise I won't trade cuddles for Facebook
I won't be ignoring you when you're upset
Because I'm too busy shouting about how happy we are
To anyone who'll listen, over the internet

I promise my social media will be quiet for now
My WhatsApp chats are mostly on hold
Watching you grow through my eyes instead of a camera lens
That's my idea of #ParentingGoals

I promise I won't let the way the world has turned
Turn my head from you
We'll embrace technology to our advantage
But it'll never be the centre of everything we do

Through countless photos and videos
We'll capture these memories of you and us
1% will be shown off on social media
But most will go on our family gallery wall
Or in our old-fashioned photo book

I promise any messages will ping during your nap time
Your hand will be held more than my phone
We'll find balance between tradition and technology
And you'll grow up in a world of reality
In our
Happy
Family
Home.

WEEK 15

Peaceful parenting

I pull myself up on the fact that I just sighed about the never-ending war I seem to be waging against dirty nappies, poo explosions and the collateral of too many toys gifted by well-meaning visitors.

As I flit between coffee shops, singing groups and meet-ups with mum friends, I return home to watch the news about the war raging on in Ukraine and as I'm sure is the case for most people, my heart aches for them. I notice the stark separation between my experience of first-time motherhood, and that of those who are giving birth under bomb shelters and rocking their babies to sleep to the sound of gunfire. My brain can't fathom how scary it must be to experience the often-turbulent emotions of motherhood, against the backdrop of war. My health visitor did warn me not to watch the news. "You need oxytocin", she said, "to keep you happy and maintain a steady flow of milk for your baby. Watch things that make you feel happy". I understand, but I simply can't ignore how lucky I am.

I'm singing nursery rhymes, drinking coffee and praying for five minutes of peace; those in war-strewn countries are losing family members, living under the constant threat of being killed, and peace isn't on the agenda for a long while. Viewing motherhood through the grim lens of war highlights the triviality of my "problems". I pull myself up on the fact that I just sighed about the never-ending war I seem to be waging against dirty nappies, poo explosions and the collateral of too many toys gifted by well-meaning visitors. In fact, I'm embarrassed to be so lucky. I'm embarrassed to be so privileged. I'm embarrassed to have just started to fully appreciate living, once I heard about people dying. I feel guilty for putting my baby to sleep in his cot and turning on his bird and ocean sounds, whilst other babies are sleeping to the sound of gunfire. The world can be so cruel.

If the evil minds who initiate conflict could see and appreciate life through the innocent eyes of a child, I'm confident that war would not exist. How do some adults grow from innocence to evil on such a profound level? Young minds rarely fail to find joy in the simplest of things; I feel that many adults would benefit from following their lead – including myself, this week. I've been feeling stressed, which is unusual for me. Yet, as I watch the news, I note the difference between "us" and "them". How have I been feeling stressed? How have I let any of my first-world "problems" become a worry? I go home to my warm, cosy nest with my baby bundled in a soft blanket, without the constant fear of myself and my family being hit by a bomb.

Never felt guilt and luck like this before
The eyes of a parent
Serve to further highlight
The futility of war.

Motherhood Marches On

As war rages on
For Ukraine's 44 million residents
We sit back
To chat
About sleepless nights
Nappy explosions
That evil Russian president

Maternity hospitals blasted
People scrambling for food
We wonder how we
On no sleep
Have lasted
As motherhood marches on
Alongside mass murder on the news

Troops puppeteered into
Firing
Taunting
Terrorising
Whilst we're complaining
About the need for five minutes' peace
About gas and petrol prices rising

Russia's running out of troops now
Soldiers mourn comrades
Those who didn't live
Whilst Putin turns
To retired veterans
To the over 50s
Just like Hitler did

This war is relentless
This greedy president
He doesn't hold back
History repeats itself
Through echoes of Chernobyl
We read in the news
Of a potential chemical attack

So whilst the sun goes down
Over the bomb-blasted city of Kyiv
I put my son down
With a full tummy
After singing him to sleep
All the while, I'm filled with gratitude
That he knows of nothing but peace

These scenes
Remind me
To bloom where I am planted
With a heart full of thanks
I'll never again take my privileged life
My comfortable motherhood
For granted.

WEEK 16

Please don't call me "Mama"

As she's talking, I see the problem without looking for it. People have been calling her "Mama".

One of the first things my highly sensitive cringe reflex cringed over when I announced my pregnancy was the phrase: "You've got this, Mama", or words to that effect. I've never enjoyed being called Mama as a replacement for my name or a term of endearment by someone who is not my child. From the moment I told people about my pregnancy, that new name fell on me like a snowstorm. Everyone was calling me Mama. To be clear, I've never wanted to dissociate myself from being a mum – I love it – but the Mama name feels cutesy and I don't like the way it's become something of an overused and undervalued term of endearment. Though I understand it's not used with this purpose in mind, the more the word has continued to establish itself into the mumsy vocabulary, the more it seems to encompass a loss of identity. Perhaps surprisingly, I don't get fidgety about being re-named "Love" or "Hun"; I'm not precious about that. For me, using Mama as a substitute for someone's name, strips that person of their identity that exists beyond motherhood. I believe it's rooted in patriarchal tradition.

Nobody ever calls my baby's dad, "Dadda" as his name or a term of endearment. Can you imagine if he turned up to his building site and his colleagues were calling him "Dadda"? It simply wouldn't happen. No, he's called Jamie and he's a joiner. He's a talented hard-worker who brings visions to life in building form. He's a lover of dance music, cars, and traditional architecture. He's also a father. He's a lover of good food, cooking, and interesting plants. He's practical-minded and likes fast cars and expensive aftershave. He's also a dad. But that doesn't need to be explained in the same way as it does for me.

I may be a mama, but my name to anyone except my son, is not Mama. My name is Laura and I'm a writer. I'm a dream-chaser, a hard worker, a home-maker with independence perhaps ingrained a little too deep into my character at times, when I push people away. I'm a sister, a daughter, a reliable friend, a fiancé. I'm a peace-chaser, a homegirl, a sun worshipper, a lover of acoustic music, crystals, and Alan Titchmarsh. Sometimes I talk too much. I'm a chocolate scoffer, a cocktail lover, and a bookworm. I like flowers, interior design and books. And yes, I'm my baby's mother – but please, don't call me Mama.

Today, one of my friends who is a single mum and conceived her baby via IVF, tells me it feels like she's lost her identity since she became a mum. She used to be the one her friends turned to when they needed help and she loved that. Now, they look straight through her because they can't see past her motherhood status. They don't include her in their plans as they used to. They don't possess the patience to see past her tired eyes and give her the time to be herself again. She just needs someone to help her unpick the tightly woven threads of motherhood slightly, so she can peep through the gaps and see that her pre-baby self is still there, shining away. As she's talking, I see the problem without looking for it: people have been calling her "Mama".

I feel sad for her because I can hear the disappointment in her voice and her desperation to reclaim a segment of her former self. I can tell that she feels like she's lost herself, though I know that she just needs to dig a little deeper beneath the surface of nappies and nap times to see that she's been here all along. This is just a season; a season where she's living in a foggy climate. I didn't meet this friend before she became a mum, yet even as a newcomer to her life, I see so many facets to this lady that she says she's lost. I see she's an independent woman who is raising her baby alone. I try hard to picture single motherhood for myself and often give up because my brain can't comprehend it. She's also a hard-working woman who has continued to climb the career ladder despite the fact that no doubt some rungs were removed on the day she told her employer about her pregnancy.

Sadly, my friend doesn't see any of the wonderful qualities that I see shining through, because she's lost amidst the haze that I know I'm lost in a lot of the time, too. I want to tell her that I see her. I see how hard she works and how well she simultaneously raises her baby– though simply surviving motherhood would be enough. I write her a poem and realise, it's also a poem to myself, and a poem to all the other mothers who have fallen victim to becoming Mama, when they don't want to be. Please see beyond my motherhood. Please, don't call me Mama.

I See You

I see you
You say you've lost your identity
Amongst the nappies
Feeds
No sleep
It will seem that way to you but
It doesn't seem that way to me

I see you
I know your identity hasn't slipped away
Because it's in the way you work hard
The way you mother your baby
The things you do for others
And
It's in the things you say

I didn't meet the pre-mum version of you
I met the premium version instead
Before, you were a hard-working, self-sufficient woman
Now, that's all sandwiched between long days
Early mornings
Sleepless nights
Putting your baby to bed

I see you
To me, you're not solely your baby's mother
Though that would be enough
You're a homeowner
Hard worker
Big achiever
You're a diamond in the rough

You say your career is dwindling
Yet
I see you juggling two jobs

And working extra hours
You’re exactly who you once were
Except now
You're bursting with superpowers

I see you
You say motherhood makes you feel like
You’re not such an independent woman anymore
I see that woman is thriving
You just need to scratch beneath the surface
A little deeper
Than before

Because these appointments
Poorly days
Play dates
They have a life of their own
But beneath it all, you’re still you
You’re just no longer doing anything
Alone

I know it gets hard
I’m on this crazy journey, too
So I just wanted to let you know
I see you’re a wonderful mother
But above all else
I see you.

WEEK 17

The magical mind of a mum

These early days of motherhood are calling for certain elements of life to be in black and white.

Pre-pregnancy, I was an easy-breezy girl. Strong willed, strong minded, willing to stick up for myself; yet it would take a *lot* for me to care enough about something to trigger that self-defence reflex. Once my body had set about building my baby, my mind simultaneously began to build stronger limits. Cleverly, my protective instincts were naturally forming. The moment I got the positive pregnancy test, I became conscious of the fact that I was my unborn baby's mother and I had a new life to protect. Along with that new-found protective role, came my stronger boundaries and metaphorically louder voice. I'm not sure if this is a temporary or lasting result of motherhood, but I find I have very little time for "I don't mind"s and "Oh, you decide"s. I have much less time in general, in comparison to my pre-baby self. These early days of motherhood are calling for certain elements of life to be in black and white.

Unlike my pre-parental days, I can't be dealing with subliminal messages or riddle-like conversations. I've discovered that there's science behind this. There are many interesting studies about how the architecture of a mother's brain changes during pregnancy. It can last for a minimum of around two –sometimes up to six – years. The changes relate to a decrease in the volume of grey matter in the brain during pregnancy. This is said to make a woman less effective at decision-making, social skills and remembering things, yet more effective at responding to her baby's needs[5]. It makes sense. If we take one long, sweeping throwback to the days of our cavemen ancestors, I don't imagine they would've been swapping pleasantries and complimenting each other's hair whilst a bear circled their baby.

Protection mode puts innate blinkers on us, forcing us to streamline what and who we have the emotional space to deal with. I've sensed this neurological change in myself since early pregnancy, which is what triggered my research. Once I saw the blue lines on my pregnancy test, it felt like I didn't have the capacity to deal with things that I would once have paid more attention to. My mind became focussed on keeping my baby alive, instead. Clever. Sadly though, the science and stardust behind these neurological changes seems to have been minimised by society under the guise of yet another cutesy term that most "mamas" become familiar with: "mum brain". It's a throwaway comment that overlooks the magic behind the chemical changes in our brains throughout pregnancy and beyond. These chemical changes help us to protect our babies. In my eyes, it's not "mum brain"; it's science that dates back to the beginning of time. I appreciate magic like that.

Alongside my enhanced protection instincts and straight-talking approach, my reinvention tendencies went into overdrive during pregnancy. I felt this strong pull to be the mum that my growing foetus would be proud of. *"How would the mum version of me present herself?"*, I'd find myself thinking. I was keen to steer myself away from the "mumsy" stereotype, so I re-stocked my wardrobe with shorter dresses; stretchy figure-hugging fabrics, and nursing bras adorned with lace and glossy gold trims. I even reinvented my make-up. Who knew that the formulation and colour of a lipstick could say: "I might be a mum now, but I'm not Mama". The nesting in my home – as documented in week one – was in full swing from the start. I needed my interiors to remind me that I'm protected, calm, and safe. Pregnancy led me to turn down the volume of life and take those cosy levels up a notch. I haven't turned the volume dial up again ever since.

Post-birth, though my personality remains pretty calm and laid back, I'm more reactive to any perceived threats to me or my family. I become fiery, protective and outspoken at a much faster rate than before. Though I still need to re-address my boundaries sometimes, I'll be forever thankful for this demanding micro-human I've given birth to. He's equipped me with skills and qualities that I hope to take through the rest of my life. Without knowing it, he's added square edges to my rounded shoulders and swapped my polite squeak for a confident lion's roar.

Our Kingdom

On the night we found about you
A new version of me was born
I grew stronger
I built boundaries

Already protecting my young

I wasn't "just" myself anymore
I became my unborn baby's mother
I developed my best-self for you
I stood taller
I grew prouder

Then you came along
As did a sense of protection I'd never felt before
You took my polite mouse squeak
Transformed it
Into a lion's roar

You took my rounded shoulders
Made the edges square
Whatever's thrown my way
I find I'm now suddenly
Prepared

You took my humble home
Turned it into our kingdom filled with love
Our spot on the sofa
Is pride rock
Where I feed my baby lion cub

Now a protective lioness
I patrol our kingdom's perimeters
Suddenly lacking in second chances
Running low
On forgiveness

Maybe one day when you're grown
My shoulders will round-out again
Memories of our kingdom might begin to fade
Yet I hope the pride, strength
And courage you've given me

Will forever
And ever remain.

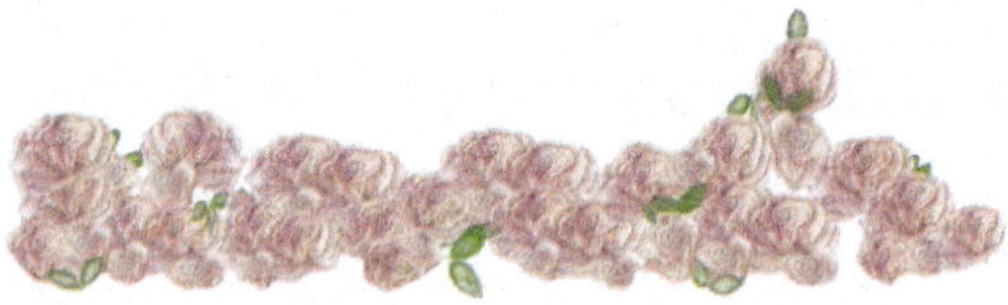

WEEK 18

Loving you, loving me

My pregnancy body may be slowly fading, but every now and again, it winks at me and reminds me of the miracle it made.

Before the birth, my entire body bloated like Veruca Salt when she turned into a blueberry, or Peter Rabbit when all his buttons popped off his waistcoat. In fact, I had a pale blue dress that made me look exactly like Peter Rabbit with his bulging buttons after one too many radishes. I'm not referring solely to what was my soon-to-be-a-mummy tummy, but to that bloat that all pregnant women seem to get from our fingers to our toes and even our lips, when our bodies are coursing with hormones to help protect and birth our babies.

My body intuitively morphed in and out, out and in, like a perfectly programmed machine, even though it had never done that before. It simply knew what to do. What a miracle. I see that now. My tummy looked like a popped blister after the birth yet I admire how, with time, my body has found its post-pregnancy silhouette. I find I respect it more than I did before. In fact, I respect *myself* more since becoming a mum. There's something about loving my baby, this extension of me, that's made me fully love myself, for the first time ever. I respect my body for creating my tiny best friend, and I respect myself for being his proud mum. My teenage self wouldn't have believed me if I told her I'd found this level of admiration for her body.

I hope my C-section scar never fades. I'm lucky to carry a hallmark of my pregnancy and birth with me for the rest of my life. The scar draws forth all the memories of those few days, when time stood still and my relationship with Jamie grew deeper, linking us forever through the ethereal experience of bringing a baby into the world. The joy, the panic, the tears, the jokes between contractions, the laughter. The scar reminds me of all those moments, in a single glance. I see it turning purple and pray that it never turns silver before disappearing completely, as scars often do.

When I'm in a yoga pose and my tummy wrinkles, I remember the way it stretched out to accommodate my bump. When I'm bloated, I can see an obvious separation in my stomach muscles. The tummy button area feels hollow, just as it did when my body carried my baby. What a privilege to see that again. My pregnancy body may be slowly fading, but every now and again, it winks at me and reminds me of the miracle it made. I've lost weight, my face has changed shape, my bum seems smaller and I'm not used to seeing big boobs on my small frame. I once dreamed of a pair like this but actually, they don't suit me at all.

I'm thankful for the "relaxin" hormone that once loosened and stretched my muscles and ligaments[6] to accommodate the growth of this new life. It certainly did make my skin do some relaxin' there for a while, though everything seems to be finding its new normal now. I look exhausted a lot of the time, because my body is taking every last nutrient I have and feeding it to my baby. Severe sickness hijacked much of my pregnancy, yet I was happier than ever before. My PMDD, for the first time in my adult life, was non-existent. I couldn't hold anything down. Now, when I put my baby down to sleep, I'm thankful for those morning sickness hormones. Look at what my body has gifted me with. My baby can knock me over, change my body, and challenge me as much as he likes. My life has changed in the best way possible.

Sorry, Mummy

Show me the world, Mummy
But don't leave me alone
It makes my tummy feel all funny
You're who I call "home"

Sorry to make you tired
I don't know about being sleep deprived
Navigating this place is a big deal
When you've recently arrived

I don't mean to cry as your food appears
It's just I need feeding, too
Hunger in my tummy is like
How heartbreak feels to you

I'm not here to manipulate you, Mummy

My mind hasn't learned that yet
I don't realise I'm stopping you from sleeping
Eating
Drinking
When I start to get upset

Sorry to disturb your conversations, Mummy
Crying is the only communication I know
And there's a lot to say through screaming
When you've this many emotions to show

Sorry for pulling your hair, Mummy
My hands have just learned how to hold
I won't understand that it hurts you
No matter how many times I'm told

One day, if I have a little one
Maybe then I'll learn, too
That I don't need to be sorry at all because
You love
Having me
At the centre of everything you do.

WEEK 19

Moving into a shed with a baby

Jamie built this temporary living space for us at the top of the garden of our soon-to-be new home. Now he can send the new house on the same journey as my baby-making body has been on: knock bits down, build bits up, make bits larger.

I've created my humble home, nested in it since week two of pregnancy, created a palatial, cosy place to bring my baby home to and today, we moved into a shed. Well, it's a lot fancier than a shed; more of a garden room. Jamie built this temporary living space for us in the garden of our soon-to-be new home. Now he can send the new house on the same journey as my baby-making body has been on: knock bits down, build bits up and make bits larger. Knowing my need for calming, familiar interiors and the mermaid-esque amount of time I spend in the bath, he's built us the most beautiful den with pared-back versions of everything we – or, let's be honest, *I* – need. It features a living room with TV mounted on the plasterboard wall, a kitchenette, a double bedroom with our baby's next-to-me cot set up just as it was at my old home; and a bathroom kitted out with a bath that we found on the side of a road. One man's trash is indeed another's treasure.

It's a glorified shed, but very fancy as far as garden rooms go and I feel lucky to have such a sophisticated space to temporarily live in. As much as we love our parents on both sides, we agree that we couldn't move in with either of them. We're too used to our independence and we have a baby now. As cringey as it sounds, our family of three is our home. So, we settle into our new accommodation where we're likely to live for the next 10-12 months. At least the cheap rough carpet will keep our feet smooth? I'm excited for the adventure, though I'm sure making boil-a-baths with an urn will be tricky at times.

I admire Jamie for the way he's gone about planning this phase of our lives. There's something about seeing him working hard and having little time for anything else – just pure, emotionless focus – before springing back to life when he gets home. I find that fascinating. I note the way he softens when he sees his family and the emotion he's poured into building our temporary shed-home. I'm grateful for the way he set up the living room just as we had it at my old house. He didn't do this because he cares how our living room is set up, but because he cares about us. I appreciate the way he drew out the plans for our new kitchen in our soon-to-be-home, not featuring the old smelly off-cut oak chopping board he treated as treasure at his old house, but to feature a step which he tells our baby is "specially for you to stand on when you bake cakes with Mummy". He's strong, emotionless and inherently masculine. Then he takes off his dusty work pants and becomes Daddy; my best friend, teammate and soulmate.

He once said that it had been his dream to have a secure, happy family and build a home for them, but never thought he'd find "the one" to do that with. I feel grateful to have been the missing piece of his jigsaw because there's no one else I could do this adventure with; no one else who would have understood the way my mind works quite like he does – particularly in the throes of PMDD. I feel thankful to both our separate pasts for breaking us down and building us up, ready for this life we've built.

Plus, I'm grateful in many ways for my propensity for ending relationships because, as Jamie said, "without my past and your past, we never would have found each other". He's right. After spending my twenties falling in love hard and fast, then breaking those relationships up again just as quick, this settled and content feeling is fairly new to me. To be thriving in love after having such a tumultuous relationship with… well, relationships, feels like a victory that I want to soak up every second of. Many will be used to this feeling I'm sure, but it's something I appreciate every day and will never take for granted. That's not to say it hasn't been hard. We've sometimes struggled finding our new flow as we get to grips with early parenthood, particularly now that we've moved into a garden room. But when parenthood brings us a storm, we hold hands through it.

Life continues to throw bricks at us sometimes, as it does for everyone, but what matters is that we're repurposing those bricks to, once again, build a fortress. Except this time, Jamie is literally building that fortress. Brick by brick and truss by truss, as our home is built and bolstered, so is our relationship and our family dynamic. You can't go through an experience like this with someone without either breaking up or becoming stronger. Thankfully, we've experienced the latter.

My Teammate

They say that having a baby
Can tear a couple apart
Sometimes, it makes you stronger
We've proven we're built from steel
On this crazy-funny-tiring
Journey of ours

The night my waters broke, you built us a den
"We'll stay up all night watching Downton", you promised
As you set about building comfort
Normality
Safety
You knew exactly what I needed
Right there and then

I expected you'd be willing me to sleep
But you embraced the adventure we were on
As we pulled an all-nighter in our labour den
I've honestly never felt more understood
By anyone

My waters broke and I jumped up in a panic
My face filled the toilet bowl with cries and groans
"It's okay", you said, calmly
As I remembered from your voice
That you're my grounding force
My teammate
My home

No one expected that labour of love
To last that amount of time
54 waking hours and you took it all in your stride
You even listened on repeat
To that soppy, acoustic
Playlist of mine

Our first night back from the hospital
I'm screaming into the mattress
Worst pain I've ever had
"How do you feel and where does it hurt?", you asked
Until you
Saw
The pain
"Oh dear", you said, "*that* bad"

Baby over your shoulder
You scooped me up to change my position
Chatting to my mum with worry in your voice
Me in one arm, a new life in the other, phone under your jaw
But you just needed somebody else to listen
You were a tired, emotional new dad
Yet, still a dedicated soulmate on a mission

"That labour followed by an emergency section
Your body's been through a LOT"
I see panic peppering your supportive words
As you stroke my hair
Pop me some pills
Then prop my feet up on a Christmas present box

And this was one of many times
When I saw my hero in you
Dedicating your everything to me
After all you
As a supporter
A provider
A new father
Had just been through

No turning over in bed
No switching off the light
Being there for me as each fragmented day
Blended from morning

To noon
Then night

I think fondly of those days
Though it was at once a euphoric and unsettling time
I often think:
How lucky am I?
To have this dedicated forever-friend
This calm
Protective
Baby-daddy
Of mine.

WEEK 20

Motherhood contradictions

The bags under my eyes tell a tale of wholesome memories built with my baby, yet they also signify how much I've lost myself.

Isn't this journey full of contradictions? Bitter-sweet, awfully-good, oxymoronic contradictions. I've prayed for sleep, then spent these early days staying awake to check-in on my sleeping baby. I've dreamt of help, then turned down any offers of a helping hand, because I'm so addicted to this little love and don't like the thought of spending time without him – even if that's just for a quick shower. I've felt overwhelmed by the changes happening in my body, then found myself wishing some remnants of the pregnancy and birth will remain forever. *Please* stay, C-section scar. Leave the blemish-fading oil in the bedside drawer, because I hope this trophy never fully fades. The little line across my lower stomach will help me to preserve this profound period of my life within the snow globe of my memory.

The contradictions continue. I'm desperately wanting to drink coffee again after being repulsed by it through pregnancy. It'd give me that feel for my old routine. Yet, the very thought of drinking a latte *still* somehow turns my stomach. Who am I? I dream of not having to share my boobs with my baby. I feel that'd help me to regain my sense of self by reclaiming my body. I wonder if the mummy sheep on *Countryfile* feels a loss of identity as they're clambered over, pulled on, and fought for by their newborn flocks? I feel for those mummy sheep. I find it exhausting feeding one life from my own body, so can't imagine how drained she must feel. Though, at least she doesn't need to concern herself with feeding-friendly clothes. I'd love to wear something all white, fluffy and cosy that lends itself to constant easy access. Still, I love feeding my baby and feel lucky to be able to do so. Being the only person who can comfort him is all-at-once beautiful and exhausting.

This hazy new motherhood experience has me wondering if I'll ever have the opportunity to do "normal world" activities again, like the lavish baths that used to make me feel like me. While some live for holidays and lavish nights out, I share that level of excitement towards a boujee bath filled with candles and a *Lush* bubble bar. It's the simple things. Now it seems I'm not within touching distance of that version of me, because when someone offers to look after my baby whilst I bathe, I have this overwhelming feeling of repulsion at the very idea of a soothing tub of bubbles. Beyond the fact that it feels as though the warm water would soak my stitches open, it feels like I leave my heart wherever my son is and even leaving it downstairs in his moses basket is too much of a distance at the moment.

Clearly, the wonderfully weird blend of disjointed emotions didn't end at pregnancy. My postnatal body is still coursing with hormones that evidently make all aspects of my post-pregnancy life feel both unsettling yet profound. The bags under my eyes tell a tale of wholesome memories built with my baby, yet they also signify how much I've lost myself. I've grown familiar with the fact that these spurts of uncertainty won't last forever, so I melt into the journey and see where it naturally takes me. Despite outside pressures to socialise and take my boy here, there, and everywhere, I know it's okay to put myself and my family first at the moment. I'm not sure how long this hazy, limbo-like period will last, but just like pregnancy and birth, I trust that my body and baby will know what to do. They'll signal when it's the natural time to move onto the next short episode of life. Being led by my baby and my instincts is, for me, the calmest way to navigate motherhood.

Motherhood Is the Best

Motherhood is preparing food whilst balancing baby on one knee
Thinking about a session of exercise
Then realising you haven't sat down
Probably already done, say…
Three?

Motherhood is praying for sleep
Then staying awake to check on your baby
It's swapping duvet days for playgroups
The excitement of 30 minutes of "peace"
That's spent fast-forwarding errands to level: crazy

Motherhood is trying to keep your identity
Then realising you've lost yourself for now
It's brushing your teeth and wet hair all at once
Hoping no one visits because
You've no hands left to hold up a towel

Motherhood is blowing raspberries whilst you clean the kitchen
It's turning every daily task into a game
It's dancing around the vacuum whilst you're cleaning
All in the name of keeping your little one entertained

Motherhood is multitasking
It's the quickest self-care ever
Motherhood is being one step ahead of everybody else
It's being the glue that holds your family together

Motherhood is the best job you've ever had
But the hours are relentless
You're working day and night shifts now
And these rolling hours seem endless

Motherhood is rediscovering yourself
It's your body confidence being thrown into doubt
And if you breastfeed
It's putting your favourite roll neck dress on
Then realising you need to get a boob out

Motherhood is slowly taking the carrier off
You've lowered yourself down on your back
Trying to remove your baby gently
Without waking them
Now they look like a flatpack

Motherhood is having your hair pulled
It's having your neck skin twisted
It's realising you're being kicked a lot of the time
But to this little person, you're beyond addicted

Motherhood is full of contradictions
Motherhood is the definition of no rest
Motherhood is having your life thrown into doubt
Motherhood is the best.

WEEK 21

The mum-shaming society

It's the boundary-breaking, patience-testing, tolerance-stretching behaviour that mums are required to brush off with elegance and a smile.

Mum-shaming. It sounds harmless, doesn't it? It was today's topic of conversation when I found myself in an enlightening chat with a group of fellow mums. As the conversation developed, I realised that I wasn't alone in the uncomfortable feelings I've been experiencing for a while, around certain people. These feelings are actually a natural response to being mum-shamed. I couldn't see what was happening to begin with, because mum-shaming isn't always immediately recognisable. In my experience, it doesn't come from a bully with a mean face. It's delivered by a soft-looking lady in a nice blouse, her comment often framed with a warm smile.

It turns out, I'm not alone. Each new mum in today's chat has confessed to feeling the same. Plus, I see it on social media, I see it in cafés and I see it at baby classes. My peers and I appear to be mothering amidst a bullying pandemic, though it flies largely under the radar because mum-shaming is bullying that's been dressed in flowers and sealed with a smile. Its ability to live under unsuspecting guises can make it tricky to spot. Mum-shaming is shaming a woman who is likely in the most vulnerable time of her life, but pre-fixing it with the word "mum", to make it sound cute.

Being mum-shamed is the snigger around the table when you're asked a judgement-laden question and falter to find a response, because you're taken aback by the sudden demand to justify your motherly decisions. It's the sly comment that encourages everyone to look at you to see your reaction. It's the brash statements that make you recoil into yourself, because *you know* that you know best, but these mum-shamers are hell-bent on making you feel otherwise. It's the pushy comments that make you want to scream: "Are *you* going to sit up breastfeeding my baby all night when our routine is off because we've worked to *your* schedule, that works for *you* and nobody else?" It's the boundary-breaking, patience-testing, tolerance-stretching behaviour that mums are required to brush off with elegance and a smile – after no sleep, no food, no shower, no "me time" and certainly, no time for this. Particularly not from a woman who's had her full eight hours of sleep or more.

I say "woman" because, in my experience and that of other mums in today's conversation, this unkindness does seem to stem from my own gender. Most notably for us, it comes from women in the generation above us. In an article published by Sheer Luxe, it's noted that "the strange thing about mum-shaming is the fact that it actually tends to be *mothers* that are the ones doing the shaming – the ones who have likely experienced criticism themselves".[7] Maybe these women have insecurities relating to the way they looked after their own offspring? Or perhaps they feel threatened by the matriarchal baton being automatically passed down to another woman once she has a baby?

Once a new family is born, it's often their home that becomes the hub of warmth and activity. Whilst I've noticed that most of "Generation X" seem happy – even relieved or excited – by this shift in focus, others appear to feel pushed out or threatened by it. I believe it's important to extend an understanding hand to these people and help them to feel included. It must be a huge culture change, which no doubt feels unsettling. Importantly though, feeling pushed out or unsettled is never an excuse to consistently treat someone else unkindly – particularly, when that someone is at their most vulnerable. Nobody should face shaming; certainly not when they need nothing but love and support.

New mums are often in such an overwhelming place after giving birth, that standing up to the shamers is last on our priority list. Likewise, onlookers don't stand against it because society is somehow wired to believe that unkindness is okay when geared towards female parents. It's become so commonplace, that no one bats an eyelid. So, we continue mothering the best we can, dodging bullets from the shamers along the way and accepting that these uncomfortable feelings are yet another rite of passage in the making of a mother.

As outlined on the BBC website, a bully is "a person who habitually seeks to harm or intimidate those whom they perceive as vulnerable".[8] You don't get much more vulnerable than new motherhood – and those who have been there before us should know that. How is shaming somebody unacceptable in the eyes of society, whereas "mum-shaming" someone during one of the most vulnerable times of her life is widely accepted? Why is shaming considered okay, just because it has the word "mum" in front of it? I'm lucky to come from a line of strong and empathetic women who cheer me along every step of the way throughout motherhood. On the tough days, they throw themselves into the thick of it with me and I've never once felt judged, watched, or looked down upon by them. Yet, I've also faced the wrath of those who try to make my motherhood about themselves – the ones who either won't, or don't know how to kindly support a new mum.

In my experience, it takes a while to pinpoint this problem. It begins as an uneasy feeling around someone who makes subtle digs about how we parent our children or throws demands on our time and expects us to conform to them. Next, our lack of reaction to the unkind comments intensifies the gravity of what's being said. These women seem not to know how to express themselves or their feelings eloquently, so eventually, when their comments haven't garnered the reaction they hoped for, their words grow legs and rip through our relationships until it feels awkward and unnatural to be around each other. Sometimes, this unpleasant evolution of mum-shaming leads to only one solution – to distance ourselves, if only for a short while, for the sake of our own health and happiness and the health and happiness of our children. Happy parent, happy baby. I'm not sure how a relationship can ever fully survive one-way unkindness and a lack of support.

Why do the shamers feel compelled to act unkindly instead of nurturing supportive relationships? Do they know they're doing it? Mum-shaming "is usually an exercise in taking the anxiety that a mother feels about her own child and deflecting it onto someone else's child", says Sheer Luxe. It seems motherhood is such a universal topic that it can make vulnerable mothers feel passionate about certain mothering choices. Does judging another mum make them feel bigger, as it brings about a fresh sense of relevance and importance in the world of motherhood? Perhaps that's a feeling they missed out on throughout their own early motherhood years. In my eyes, a woman who tries to heal her own wounds by taking her hurt out on the generation of mothers who she should be setting a kind example for, is not, no matter how it's dressed up, a safe woman to be around in the tricky early days of new motherhood. And so, many women are choosing distance and peace, instead – before getting mum-shamed for that, too.

Whilst I try to understand the psychology behind shaming, I believe those who do it, need to heal their wounds from the inside and not deflect their hurt onto younger parents. Some mums in today's chat confided that they've found themselves grappling with this form of bullying from close family members or friends who they once had a strong relationship with. For a couple of them, it's reached a point where they felt they've had no choice but to cut-off their friends, in-laws, even their grandparents completely. There came a point when the shaming simply became too much and ending the relationship was, sadly, the only healthy way to move forward. What a shame, for the beauty of a new life to bulldoze even the strongest relationships.

I hope our generation can break this toxic loop for the sake of our children and their future families. I'm keen to bring my son up knowing that *bullying is never okay,* however it manifests itself and no matter what word is put in front of it to make it sound endearing. Bullying is just as bad coming from a smiley, perfumed lady, as it is coming from someone who looks like a stereotypical bully. When I become an older-generation mum, I won't be pelting any form of unkindness at parents who are younger than me. I won't be rolling my eyes, sarcastically laughing, or grappling to fill my empty nest or my unfulfilled time with a baby that isn't mine, or weighing in on topics that are none of my business. I vow to maintain my own identity beyond motherhood, whilst remaining open-minded, kind-hearted and forever supportive of those I love – no matter what decisions they make, or which unique parental path they choose. Whenever I hear a a person shaming a mum, I'll challenge that person and ask why they feel they have a right to comment on how another woman raises her child. Whether it's a throw-away comment or venomous remark, I will question unkindness towards new parents, always.

One strong thread that myself and the other mums in today's chat had in common, was that none of us knew the "right" way to respond to being shamed. They don't teach you this in school, yet we're all taught how to find the square root of numbers (something I've never felt compelled or required to do in my adult life so far). We agreed that we wish these women would understand that so much has changed since they had their children, so there's really no need to push their expectations onto us. Nor is there any need for unkindness or judgement. All we'd like is mutual love and support.

It’s All Changed

Our relationship, around the edges
We see it turning black
Our arms are reaching out for you
But yours aren't reaching back

Please see past our protective parenthood
And know that we still love you
But we need you as our anchor
For this pressured tide we're swimming through

Please take note
Because it seems that bit by bit
Our relationship is reaching a stage
Where it’d be healthier to turn our back on it

We know you might like to be more involved
To sweep our babies away for the day
We understand that if you were in control
You’d perhaps do things a different way

You may want to refill your empty nest
You might like to relive your motherhood
But please back off when we ask you
Not to do any of this through us

You see, this is our time now
We’ve learned different tips and tricks
And the best thing you can do
Is just let us get on with it

We struggle to convey this
We’re sleep deprived
Too tired to word it any better
Let’s write it down to capture these thoughts
I'll write you a letter.

To those who try to break our boundaries

Evidently, motherhood has transformed a lot since you were a new parent. We're not sure what the maternal landscape looked like then, but please accept that a lot of it has shifted. We don't always want to hand our babies over so you can look after them whilst we do A and B and C, and X and Y and Z. This is our hard-but-short season of parenthood and we're throwing ourselves into it. In fact, we'd like to preserve these moments between the dreamy, watercolour pages of a fairytale so we can revisit them for infinity.

Some mums may yearn for a day to themselves; others would prefer to stay close to their little ones. Some mums believe it takes a village to raise a child; others prefer a hamlet, or a small circle. Please respect each mother's preference. Some of us don't want de-babying for long stretches of time – if at all – and that's our choice. Thank you for the offers but if we say "no", please respect that, as our choice, informed by our instincts. No need to roll your eyes. We won't flex, morph and bend until we find a compromise that suits you. We will continue to set our boundaries, no matter how many attempts are made to break them.

We understand you might like to look after our little ones on your own; to squish them, cuddle them, bathe them, feed them treats, put them to bed and wake up with them on Christmas morning. Please understand, this can be a lot to ask from a new family who are making their own traditions now; just as you once had the opportunity to do when you were a new parent. Here's the bit that may be hard to read –

This time, it's not about you.
You had your time.

A lot has changed since you had your time, so please don't push your expectations on us. It's hard enough navigating the minefield of motherhood, without outdated information or demands being thrown into the mix. Please refrain from telling us that we shouldn't contact nap and how to put our babies down in their cots. Stop asking when we'll wake them or why we haven't done something to your specification. It's not your job this time. If you don't appreciate our parenting techniques, turn your attention to something else.

Please refrain from asking when we're going to stop breast or bottle feeding. Do you really need to know when our babies are going to be weaned? Asking on a regular basis brings unnecessary pressure. The answer is probably "I don't know; I'm led by my baby". That will continue to be the answer, no matter how many times you ask that question.

Our babies don't exist as your new hobby or career. Of course, we'd like our little love to enhance your life and for you to play a key role in theirs – but you should fit into their life and not the other way around. If you feel pushed out, bored, or lonely, please focus on healing yourself from the inside because that's not our wound to heal, nor our gap to fill.

We understand that it's not always us you want to see anymore. Once a baby arrives, it's naturally them you might want to spend time with. We'll happily step out of the spotlight, but we won't be removed from the wings. We'd like you to welcome us *all*, as a family, rather than making the new parent feel like the chauffeur who should wait outside.

There's no need to make "you don't know how easy you have it" comments. It's not a competition. Yes, easy access to a washing machine and disposable nappies streamlines life, no doubt; but you had it easier in other ways. You haven't experienced being in the generation of new mums who are drowning under the pressure of conforming to tradition whilst also flourishing as modern women. Perhaps you weren't expected to be a mum, a housekeeper *and* climb a career ladder where, since you got pregnant, most of the rungs were removed?

We'd love for you to care for us as you did before. If you can't offer an understanding hand at the time when we need it the most, your hand will be pushed away. Happy parents, happy baby. By loving us, you're loving our little ones and by loving us both, can you imagine how our relationship could flourish?

WEEK 22

A fresh perspective

No more tripping over the suitcase as I stumble into the bathroom to take a paracetamol and have a bath, in the hope my hangover won't be too bad. Leave the gin downstairs – this is just the tonic.

We're spending a weekend away in the countryside at a reunion of family and friends. As we pull up on the gravel driveway, I'm struck by how calm, content and blissfully happy I feel. Must be week four of my menstrual cycle – what a happy coincidence. This is the week I look forward to each month. The one that makes me wish, so desperately, that I could fully break free from PMDD because, though the monster has calmed slightly since my diagnosis, I don't want to feel homesick for this joy when he comes back next week. I'm pleased to be able to fully enjoy this break with clear, content eyes and a happy heart.

The feeling of being on our first trip away as a new family enhances this happiness. Through my teens and twenties, I still felt like a child at events like this. I'd usually be nursing a hangover or a broken heart from yet another breakup. This time, as I unclip my baby from his car seat, I'm struck by how wholesome it feels to arrive as a family. For me, motherhood, just like childhood, teenagehood and non-motherhood adulthood, has become a phase all of its own. I love seeing life through these new-mum lenses. Sometimes it seems as though I'm looking through someone else's glasses.

Maybe it's because I'm not accustomed to the luxury of a floor that doesn't creak as it does in the makeshift shed that we call home, or maybe it's the splendour of having a bath that has taps rather than the cumbersome twisty knob on our boil-a-bath contraption. Perhaps it's the lavish bath and body oils infused with all sorts of botanicals. I'm enjoying seeing this break from a different perspective than usual: chatting with a prosecco isn't my priority. Swishing through the meadow of flowers outside and introducing my baby to the bees and buttercups takes precedence now. I love this fresh perspective.

It's a few hours later and the clock has ticked around to early evening. I've socialised a lot, but I no longer linger in the hazy bar, inhaling the alcohol fumes and slightly musty cologne that follows the evening meal. There was a period of my life where, by the time I made it to the bedroom at an event like this, I'd be seeing everything in double-vision. This time, I'm noticing the fluffiness of the towels and the fresh, crisp feel of the starched sheets.

I used to think attending this kind of event with a baby would involve putting the little ankle biter to bed with a monitor and going back downstairs to join the party. In reality, my baby is where my party is right now so here I am upstairs – seemingly premature, compared to my pre-baby days – enjoying the grandeur of our roomy family bedroom. I'm swishing my son around in the bath and watching him giggle under the dimmed lights whilst my tea brews on the side. For the first time in my life, I see the pleasure of staying somewhere like this through fully sober, fresh eyes. No more tripping over the suitcase as I stumble into the bathroom to take a paracetamol and have a bath, in the hope my hangover won't be too bad. Leave the gin downstairs – this is just the tonic.

I find wholesome happiness in making my son comfy, as I apply cream to each dainty fold of his neck after cuddling him in the soft, fluffy white hotel towel. I'm tucking his tiny feet comfortably into his koala-printed sleepsuit as I note the resemblance between the koalas and him. How did nature make this little person so cute? All the while, his peach-toned salamander arms throw upwards towards me, begging to be picked up again. All he wants is a hug. I snap the last popper into place and carry my little koala over my shoulder, grinding my teeth at the cuteness of his tiny bottom in his pyjamas.

Noting the murmur of everyone socialising downstairs, the slightly dull, muffled voices form an underscore to our slow dance around the bedroom as I rock my baby to sleep. I don't resent anyone for being down there. I love being here, whilst his dad holds the forte for our family's social side. I clamber into the fresh sheets of the hotel bed and fluff up the comfy pillows, taking a sip from my now-cold tea as I feed my baby and he acts like he hasn't had a drink since 1982. Pulling the crisp covers over my legs, I watch his eyes getting heavier and heavier, until his head flops gently to the side. Asleep. If bliss could be bottled, I'd ditch our cases and pack the boot with this takeaway happiness.

I'll fully immerse myself into this freedom. The bliss of our first family holiday, free from the shackles of PMDD. I'll find joy in every abstract piece of art that makes up my life. Because I know that next week, no matter how much I practice mindfulness and gratitude, the monster will slop himself out of the sewer, ready to fill my head, heart, feelings and entire body with the destructive, carcinogenic tar I've become so accustomed to.

The Wholesome Life

This journey is ups and downs
So I embrace the ups
I point out the bees
The rolling hills
The dancing buttercups

Weeping willow trees
Fields of grazing cows
And sweet lambs
Chewing grass
In their sweet little mouths

I have time to notice nature
Though there's no time left for me
What a delightful contradiction
Fast is meeting slow and
It's my favourite way to be

I used to rush through life
Barely even noticing
Now my tired eyes have time
To see the spring buds open
To watch the sunrise and hear the starling

No socialising at the bar this time
No more inhaling musky cologne
Wherever my baby is
That's the place for me

I'll call it home

I've swapped back-to-back meetings
And headaches over spreadsheets
For a form of exhaustion
That's swallowed by long walks
Smelling fresh dough at the bakery

What a form of abstract torture
Yet, what a mindful way to be
As I melt my tired body into nature
I realise
This wholesome life is made for me.

WEEK 23

Parenting with a heavy heart

The sticky hand of PMDD is beckoning, summoning my entire body and brain with taunting thoughts. This is the dark side of having a mind like this.

I've been practising mindfulness and gratitude. I've thanked my lucky stars for the privilege of bringing my baby up in a peaceful country. I've played *The Glad Game* a million times over, embracing every single thing I'm grateful for. But it's back. PMDD doesn't acknowledge positive thinking, "cheer up" advice, or mindfulness diaries. So, my happy mind is flung back into the depths of darkness, and all I can do now is steady myself by holding on to the rollercoaster. I know it will stop. It always does. It's just a matter of when.

I'm at the peak of the exhaustion – the most wonderful kind of exhaustion, as we all hasten to add – of motherhood. The sticky hand of PMDD is beckoning, summoning my entire body and brain with taunting thoughts. This is the dark side of having a mind like this. This monster rampages through my brain, pickling it with misplaced guilt about every social interaction I had that day; categorising people, comments and plans as good/bad, safe/unsafe on this obsessive journey to protect myself from anything that may cause my heart to be jolted and dropped into the depths of that dark, lonely place.

They say that labelling your thoughts is good for mindfulness, but with a mind like this, you sometimes run out of labels in your label maker. Because nothing can ever just "be" when I feel like this. Everything has significance, no matter how hard I try to detach myself. From an onlooker's perspective, how useless it must seem, to sit here, picking everything apart so negatively. This isn't my hobby. I pride myself on my optimism, when I'm able to be myself and not this hi-jacked, foggy version of me. When this monster slops itself out of the tar-filled sewer and strangles my brain, I become a pessimist, trapped in a happy person's body. I'm sifting the "good" from the "bad" in a genuine, rushed panic to protect myself. I magnify the most infinitesimal "problem" and feel so grief-stricken by it, until that tiny snag in my jumper becomes a loop, which droops further until it creates another loose loop – then eventually unravels the entire knit. The threat of what might happen when I'm off guard seems more daunting than the process of protecting myself. This is how I end up retreating from friends, family and plans. My mind doesn't have the space for a single thing more.

Eventually, I've soaked up my maximum capacity of toxic thoughts and the monster sets his sights upon my body, instead. This is when the physical exhaustion sets in. Those poisonous feelings seep out of my brain like thick, sticky tar and run through my physical self, lighting up a burning, heavy ache through each muscle, tendon, and limb. A psychological reaction that creates a physical, suffocated feeling, making me gag on the piercing pain of every stinging thought and feeling.

Once, I would have slept and slept and slept it off until I could function again. Now, I cry and cry and cry in silence, whilst my baby thrashes and feeds. Because there's no time for your needs when you're striving to create a flawless life for your little one. That's when I feel comfort. I realise I've found a tonic. The bottomless pit does, this time, have a floor. I look at my baby and am shocked into a refreshing consciousness. He guides me into a sparkling world of innocence, which nobody's ever shown me before.

He'll never know it. It would be unhealthy for me to pin my adulthood pain onto his tiny, innocent shoulders. These are my problems to fix. Yet, my son unknowingly leads me into a magic painting book; one swish of the water-dipped paint brush and my black and white world is awash with colour and light. The trees that once stood bare and grey are given luscious leaves. They're given movement. They swish and sway next to blossom trees, bursting with blush pink prettiness. The frozen stream that once sat stagnant and forgotten, is now flowing freely and glinting in the sun. For each baby class we attend, each nursery rhyme we sing, each glossy page we turn in his books, I'm grateful for the glimpse of pure, undiluted innocence and happiness. Everything is going to be okay.

The Monster Returns

Back again
This monster
Swears it'll never leave me

Sludges over from the sewer
Threatens to snatch me from my family

Its grip tightens around my wrist
Promises to take me under
To a place I've been where white is black
Where sunshine looks like thunder

Where rainbows are grey
And birds don't tweet
Where flowers never bloom
And sweets aren't sweet

Friends say I'm always happy
And confident and positive
Look at me now
Everything's on hold and
It hurts to even exist

Baby's dad leaves for work
Please don't go
His presence helps to keep this devil at bay
But how does a grown woman explain to a man
That he's helping to keep a monster away?

So I say goodbye and sit alone
Familiar with what comes next
The monster sets a snake upon my heart
Wraps itself around my neck

My brain's under attack – he's back
I'm haunted by a million thoughts
I beg it to please give me some rest
Before the pressure of a thousand bricks
Falls onto my chest

Like a fox that's been chased to exhaustion

Shallow breaths
Lying helpless on the floor
I wonder how my struggling brain and body can cope
With even a millisecond more

As the monster slops me into its sewer
I hear a tiny cry
Thank my angels for that
I'm swept back into a world of innocence –
My baby's awake from his nap

You might think I couldn't mother him like this
Yet, here's a stronger version of me
I thrive in motherhood
I've grown stronger alongside my family

So I chase my baby around the room
Pretending *I'm* the scary monster
We fill the room will laughter
My baby chases the monster back
Crawling faster and faster

Then as we both collapse
A good kind of breathless this time
In a helpless ball on the floor
I realise the monster has lost his power
My baby saw him off
So he can't choke me anymore

With a little boy in my arms
And a depleted devil on my back
Motherhood marches on
And next time, when the monster returns
Here's my knight in shining armour
The beast has been tamed
Unknowingly
By my son.

WEEK 24

Happiness begins at home

I nest for every incoming tricky time, every happy time, every life event. My interior set-up correlates with my sense of content. My home is my emotional management system, my lifelong crash mat.

I've been interested in home design since I used to style showhomes with my grandma in the school holidays. I found the most exciting part of her job was receiving a treasure trove of interior decor in large cardboard boxes. Golden candelabras, snuggly throws, scatter cushions – a box of props that would help us to transform the empty room into our cosy palace. My task would be to stage the tablescapes and soft furnishings, creating a sense of grandeur with candelabras, before plumping and arranging the cushions and nonchalantly draping the throws to create the stylish kind of nest that I'd like to live in.

Grandma would take care of the bigger tasks, like hanging artwork. She'd often forgo the hammer, instead choosing to knock nails into the wall using her heel, shrouded in the scent of Chanel N°5. What a woman. I can still feel the way my mood – our moods – transformed with the room. We'd start out early in the morning, still a little tired and by the afternoon, we'd be filled with energy and excitement after having the most wholesome time. Once the room was prepped and polished, Grandma would make us what became known in our family as the famous "Grandma cup of tea"; one so sweet that it must have been saturated with a naughty amount of sugar. We'd chat for a while as though we were at her cosy home on Jack Lane, except this time we were enjoying the fruits of our labour in our self-styled palace.

To this day, the way my home is styled affects how I feel. I believe much of that is attributed to the comfort and nostalgia brought about by those times spent styling showhomes with my grandma. My affinity with interiors is also a creative by-product of my PMDD. I understand the way textures and colours can create comfort and through my hardest times with PMDD, nest-making was the only activity that brought slight relief. The pain bleeding through my body and the monster beginning to ravage my mind was my cue to set about cleaning and re-styling my home so I had a comfy place to be puppeteered by the PMDD monster. I was quite literally nesting to soften the painful blow of being so unwell. Having lost the ability to maintain friendships, relationships or even contact with close family members for a short while during my hardest bouts of PMDD, if ever the monster got to me before I'd created a nest to feel heavy feelings in, I found that period of suffering felt harder and lasted longer.

Of course, there are plenty of theories behind the instinct to nest for comfort. The popular Danish term "hygge" dates back to the 19th century, though it's recently had a resurgence and was added to the Oxford English Dictionary in 2017. Borrowed from the Old Norse language, it's said to mean "protected from the outside world". It's used to summarise the feeling of finding joy and contentment in the little parts of life – whether that's your favourite pair of socks or a hot chocolate in a sofa den with Alan Titchmarsh on the TV. At least, that's my definition of the word.

The ancient art of the Chinese Feng Shui stems even further back, to the ninth century BC. The combination of Feng (wind) and Shui (water) refers to the art of arranging your home in a way that creates harmony in your living space and results in good energy. Though the science of interior therapy highlighted in these ancient practices is often lost nowadays amidst pictures of cashmere socks in glossy coffee table books, I find it to be powerful for cultivating calm and in turn, minimising the impacts of PMDD.

If I didn't experience such deep sensitivities, I'm not sure I'd have such a keen interest in home design. If I was simply styling for the aesthetic, I believe I'd have lost interest during my last reinvention. As it happens, my love for interiors is ingrained deep within my belief system, so my passion for it has never faded. I never feel offended or embarrassed when people tell me that my home is "too tidy" or "too much like a showhome", because I know there's more to it than simply upholding the aesthetically pleasing image of a well-kept home. As mentioned in week one, I've been nesting my entire life. I nest for every incoming tricky time, every happy time, every life event. My interior set-up correlates with my sense of content. My home is my emotional management system, my lifelong crash mat.

That's why, this week in the garden room, I'm finding it hard to juggle the pressures of motherhood whilst not being in my usual, homely surroundings. It's tricky to create comfort in a glorified shed. I'm imagining what our final home will be like beyond the architectural drawings and mood boards. Though I'm enjoying our adventure under the stars, I feel homesick for that perfectly-manicured nest I'd made in my old home. Everything in this one is temporary and I feel like I'm in limbo.

I wish that my future self could tell this present version of me that living in this garden room will soon have me flourishing and blooming alongside the flowers in our new garden. It's difficult to imagine life beyond these plasterboard walls and boil-a-baths. I know that one day we'll get there and things that feel hard now, will be soothed by the interior therapy we'll create in our new home. It's just a matter of time, patience and perseverance. One day, the tricky times will once again be softened but for now, I'll hold on to the rollercoaster tightly, because this temporary living situation feels particularly hard right now.

This is Hard

This is hard
This is really hard
Navigating this beautiful
Different
Life of ours

Mothering in a shed
My teammate is building our home
A place for us to live
I'll never lose sight of how lucky I am
Never pre-empted how tricky this is

As soon as I've cleared away breakfast
Cleaned my baby's clothes and the floor
We have the lunchtime hurricane
And there's more, there's more
Then there's more

My body is beyond weary
My arms can't carry anymore
They once carried my own responsibilities

Now they're raising a human
A crucial mission I've never done before

I wonder if I'd find this easier
If we lived comfortably
In a normal home
If baby's dad wasn't working crazy hours
If I wasn't mothering our first-born on my own

I'd still struggle with the pressures
The expectations of motherhood are a lot with a mind like this
"You need to cook and clean and fluff the pillows
And surprise!
You're CEO of the Christmas and birthday gift list"

These tasks seem really simple
But I've spent most of my life building a career
Now there's a demand to share my life with others
Reassuring those who miss him
That we're here

I'm the point of contact
Everyone wants to see him
My entire world has changed
And it's a much happier –
Yet sometimes, more complicated
World to live in

I've no free time and I'm exhausted
Swimming with my head just above water
Yet all the plans and dates for the diary
Are feeling
Increasingly tougher

Just as I've replied
To the swarm of messages
More come flooding in

We've only just re-gained balance
Now we're back to this round-robin of plans again

People clambering for a piece of him
When's he free? When are you free?
When are you free to meet me
And me?
And me?
And me?

So, I turn my phone off
Time for me and my son
The real world needs to be shut out for now
Whilst we cuddle up and, just the tonic:
"Let's put a blanket and a film on".

WEEK 25

Life on Jack Lane

In fact, I decided I never wanted to start another relationship again. I was afraid of risking the wholesome happiness of enjoying my independent life on Jack Lane.

Though she was consistently by my side through the sunshine and storms of my life, my grandma sadly never learned of my diagnosis and never had the opportunity to meet my son. She passed away just a couple of years before seeing my tumultuous story's happy new beginning. This hit me harder than anything I've ever experienced. Though of course I loved her for everything she was – everything she still is – she was also the only person who somehow understood the inner workings of my brain. I believe I got my mind like this, from her.

The emotional reflection of myself, my grandma was sensitive, creative, empathetic and often fiery with her emotions. Just as I've noticed in my own mannerisms, she was partial to a reinvention. She'd revamp her image regularly and had an outfit for every imaginable occasion, though she rarely came across that occasion in real life. Her bedroom resembled a costume room from a Hollywood film. Pearl-scattered collars, clean-cut blazers, kitten heels and soft silk blouses. Elegance personified. As I journey through life, my brain loops together the parallels between Grandma and me. The good and the bad. I think about the way she cut off friends. It wasn't until her funeral that I finally met a few of them from years gone by; those I'd only ever heard about in the fond stories she shared. Just like me, my grandma enjoyed time alone, had tumultuous relationships, was fiercely independent and loved the comfort provided by a well-styled room.

In light of all our similarities, I wish I had the opportunity to share my diagnosis with her. I'd love to explore whether she, too, suffered from PMDD during her reproductive years and if that shaped her character through later life. I'm keen to know if she had a mildly neurodivergent mind. I'd do anything to show her that I've pieced together the puzzle of how to live – and even thrive – with a mind like ours. Maybe if she'd been on this learning journey with me, she wouldn't have cut all her friends and

relationships off throughout life and would have had a chance at this *lasting* feeling of wholesome happiness – as I feel that I do, post-diagnosis.
In the early days that followed my grandma's passing, grief took me to a dark place of irrational anger towards her. How could she provide such a strong sense of understanding and support, then leave me to figure everything out alone? Why did she let me love her so much that I'd reach a point where I'd feel so painfully lonely without her? I irrationally felt as though she'd been irresponsible for loving and understanding me too much, before leaving, just like that.

On that sunny spring morning when time stood still for a while as Grandma flew to Heaven, my comfort blanket, support network, and understanding hand in the confusing haze of my condition evaporated from the earth, followed by a dramatic and sudden thunderstorm to announce the departure of a precious one. I knew that my experience of the world as I knew it was about to take on a whole new shape. I'd need to unpick what my existence looked like without her. This was going to be a painful lesson in how to navigate life without the one person who understood my then-undiagnosed condition. For a long while, it felt like I was flying in a zero-oxygen chamber, unable to get a hold of who I was – or what the world was – without her here. Since she departed from earth, I've undoubtedly never returned to the "me" I was before her passing. For a long time, I felt a pressure to continue with the momentum of others as they moved forward, yet it felt as though a whole chunk of my soul had been removed and I couldn't work out how our planet seemed okay to keep orbiting the sun without her here.

In a desperate attempt to feel closer to my grandma after she passed away, I found a house close to where she lived, on an estate just off Jack Lane in Moulton, Northwich. During the build-up to my move-in date, I gathered a cardboard box of home decor, including special trinkets from her home and a few new candles and throws. On the day I moved in, I set about transforming the empty rooms into a cosy nest, just as I used to do with my grandma when we styled showhomes together. This time, it was me shrouded in the scent of her Chanel N°5 and me hammering nails into the wall with my heel. I felt like quite the woman.

Simple, humble and comforting, my home on Jack Lane became my secure nest, where I'd explore the raw and undulating throes of grief. It was also the place where I'd capture the mental clarity I needed to kickstart my quest for a diagnosis. I created what I call my "Carrie Bradshaw palace", complete with a wardrobe for my clothes and shoes – no male items hanging or sitting alongside them. I was in my element. Though grief-stricken and struggling with what I now know to be PMDD and a neurodivergent mind, moving to Jack Lane made me excited for what my new life would bring. I hit the emergency stop button on the conveyor belt of male relationships and for the first time ever, enjoyed my own, peaceful company. In fact, I decided I never wanted to start another relationship again. I was afraid of risking the wholesome happiness of enjoying my independent life on Jack Lane. A few years later, you couldn't beat the irony of me returning to No-Boys-Allowed HQ, flopping through the door as I clutched my C-section stitches with my baby boy and future husband following behind. Life does have a funny way of making a fool out of you sometimes.

I believe that through my affinity with interiors – a passion nurtured by my grandma – that home healed my heart. My independent life on Jack Lane prepared me for this current segment of my journey. I'm not sure where my grandma is now, but I often feel guided by her. I'm sure she simply needed to nest in her new home, too. She was probably unpacking her cardboard box of treasured memories alongside me. Perhaps she needed to calm her sensitive angel mind and settle her soul, before reaching back down to return my sense of gravity on earth and show me a way to live without her.

A couple of weeks before we moved into the garden room as a family of three, I woke from a short sleep to the sound of my son stirring. As I peered into his cot, something about him seemed extra comforting and familiar. Unexpectedly and for the first time, I saw my grandma's expression on his tiny face. He'd developed her dimples and her slightly side-on smile. Her physical presence may be gone, but she often finds a way to smile at me and put her comforting hand on my shoulder during my biggest life moments. For that, I'm thankful. I'll tell my baby about his angel relative until the day I become his angel mum.

Your Angel Relative

There's a special someone
Who you're just about to meet
Though her feet don't touch the earth anymore
Her soul is here, still sparkling

Everything I do for you
Every part of me you see
Is carved by a person you'll always be held by
Because her arms
They held me

Jack Lane
That's where she lives
That's where we drank tea together, chatting about
Boys
Life
How I'm too independent for relationships
But wait a minute...
Oh yes, Grandma:
One day I definitely want kids

Now here we are
That "one day" has come
And just like her in 1960
My first-born
Is a son

She'll never stop chatting
Don't stop here if it's peace
Or fine dining you're after
But you can bet you'll leave with a happy heart
And a tummy full of laughter

When they invent a phone line
And we can make a call to Heaven

You're the first topic we'll talk about
I've been telling her about boys since I was 11

I'll say "Grandma, this is a special one
He's completely stolen my heart
Because unlike the boys you've advised me on
Our bond will never fall apart"

She'd have noticed your rosebud lips
She'd have said: "Look at those little sparrow thighs"
Before proudly sobbing through her words
"He looks like you, Love
With those almond eyes"

Amidst these smiles and memories
I'll take a moment to acknowledge the pain
Because though her blood pulses through our veins
It's a shock to remember I'll never
Cuddle her
Contagiously laugh
Or drink tea with her again

And that's when the grief feels piercing
It hits me like a bus
To think that you too, might feel this one day
When it's just "you"
Instead of "us"

But I open my eyes in the morning
And her dimples and smile live on
She's right here next to me, I realise
I see her in my son.

WEEK 26

Going at our own pace

As social media buzzes along, making everyone feel the need for a Pinterest-perfect nursery and luxury holidays, I'm over here raising my baby in a shed, having never felt more rich, wholesome, and fulfilled.

I'm feeling pretty victorious this week. Still sleep deprived and exhausted, yet I seem to be striking some kind of balance that resembles normality – or the shed life version of normality. I always manage to wash my baby and my teeth, but this time, the dishes, my hair and face have also been cleaned. Following the simplicity of life through my baby's eyes, it's become all about these small wins. Plus, moving into our garden room has made me appreciate the simpler things in life. There's something about this basic sense of simplicity that strips back the smoke and mirrors of motherhood as you see it in films and across social media. Our less-than-glamorous scenario shines a sobering spotlight on what really matters. I don't need a nursery or an expensive home; I just need my family. As social media buzzes along, making everyone feel the need for a Pinterest-perfect nursery and luxury holidays, I'm over here raising my baby in a shed, having never felt more rich, wholesome, and fulfilled. Interestingly, this sense of fulfilment negates the need to post a single thing on social media.

As I see the installation of our beautiful kitchen, I don't feel compelled to show anyone except my mum. I've broken out of that toxic loop of "if you don't post it, it didn't happen" and it feels liberating. I've found a sense of wholesome adventure in living here with my family. Our journey isn't just beginning – it's already begun and I'm enjoying doing things at our own pace, rather than following the timeline that society set for us. Of course, there are also times when I struggle living here.

Sometimes, I envy others with their fancy, functioning taps and panelled walls, whilst I'm living in a make-shift plasterboard garden room with boil-a-baths and a 26-week-old baby. I'm sensitive to my surroundings and interior styling soothes my overthinking mind. Our current living arrangement couldn't be further from those comfortable days when I nested in my homemade palace for one. I wouldn't swap it, but it's hard.

The floor is so creaky that we've been memorising which boards are the noisiest, to avoid waking our baby when we go to bed. It's become a well-choreographed dance routine. I walk in sideways like a crab to avoid those two initial squeaky boards, before breaking into long, exaggerated creeps like a careful flamingo, ensuring my foot lands gently in just the right place to avoid that baby-waking creaky wood. Even so, I'm embracing this flamingo-walking, adventure we're on. One day, I'll wake up after a full night's sleep, and my arms will be empty. That's when I'll feel nostalgia for these sleep-deprived, up-in-the-air days of den-making with my family.

My Arms Will Be Empty

We still get no sleep
He's unhappy until his tiny body is encased in mine
Almost six months of thrashing, gurgling, kicking around
Until I realise I just watched the sun rise

I pull all the tools from my mothering toolkit
Feeding, patting
Walking him around for a bit
But my efforts are futile
When I put him down
Instantly, he picks up on it

Here we go
Bottom lip out, big breath in
The nappy-clad salamander is back
Skin to skin
He's perched upon my shoulder again

My body is begging for sleep
My mind is starved of peace
But as I snuggle up to these miniature shoulders
I know I wouldn't swap any of this

Our friends say they get over eight hours' sleep
But for now, my half hour is plenty

Because one day I'll wake from a restful sleep
And my arms will be empty.

WEEK 27

Mums, dads and superheroes

If we describe all the roles a doting mum fulfils in her child's life, then swap the "mum" for "dad", suddenly we've gone from "of course she does that!" to "wow, this guy is a superhero".

In one banana's time, my WhatsApp replies need to be wrapped up. In the next turn of a *That's Not My Dinosaur* page, my teeth must be brushed. In roughly 25 more bounces of the jumperoo, my hair and make-up's done whether I like it or not. My time used to be measured by a watch. Now, everything I do is counted in a variety of weird and wonderful ways. Each second needs to be used wisely and once my baby wakes, is bored, or in any other way needs attention, that's me officially considered "done", on whatever I was doing. I used to get excited to hear the sound of the ice cream van, to snuggle down with a book and a family-sized chocolate bar to myself, or to hear the wine cork pop out and glug-glug-glug into the glass. Now, sitting by myself for a moment is the novelty I get excited for. It doesn't happen often; only when Jamie is home from work and I can take my eyes off our son. That short moment to think for myself, as myself, feels like a much-needed punctuation mark in my day.

Admittedly, I feel envious of Jamie sometimes, because he gets to perch for a while, regaining the mental clarity that comes with an uninterrupted chat and a hot drink during his tea break. I wouldn't swap my situation; I love motherhood and one day I'll miss this. I embrace being with my baby and appreciate the motherly bond I have with him. Yet, sometimes, on the days when my arms don't feel like they can carry anymore, my legs are buckling beneath me and I'm falling asleep standing up, I can't help but feel envious that Jamie still gets to be Jamie and his sense of identity has never swayed. It feels like my entire sense of self has been knocked over and building myself back up is proving tricky. I haven't quite figured out who this new version of me is – nor have I had the time to. Whether it's the familiarity of working or the comfort of drinking tea, maternity-leave mums don't get to hold on to the grounding elements of routine that working fathers do.

Today, Jamie got home, took a good while in the bathroom to wash and reset, then reeled in the compliments on his fathering skills when a visitor praised him for reading our son a book. I do believe I just lost my internal final straw. I don't deny him of his glory. He's an amazing dad and I feel lucky that my son has him as his key male role model, yet our proud visitor seemed almost shocked that a father can be so attentive. If we describe all the roles a doting mum fulfils in her child's life, then swap the "mum" for "dad", suddenly we've gone from "of course she does that!" to "wow, this guy is a superhero". Of course, the same goes for any default parent – it's not always mum – but in our situation, I am the mum and default parent.

To me, Jamie was already a superhero before our baby came along. He enhances the wonderful, independent life I created; he's the black and white, straight-thinking mind to my brain bursting with colour and emotion. He was my right-hand man during pregnancy, birth and the early postnatal days. He's the practical part to my jigsaw that I've always been missing. He's encouraged me to see life in an entirely new way when I've struggled through the tricky times of PMDD. He took over everything when I was pregnant and plunged into an exhausting pit of morning sickness. He became my head chef, cleaner, counsellor, best friend, transport and maid, all in one and when I tell him that he's getting a little lost in himself whilst I'm over here losing myself, he snaps back into dedicated dad mode.

I don't deny Jamie of his first-class title, but the fact that he's heralded a hero for the simple act of reading a book to his child, shows we have a long way to go in terms of achieving equilibrium between our genders. I think Jamie's a hero, but I don't think some of the things that outsiders applaud him for, are all that heroic. It's his birthday this week and I'm celebrating him in all his facets. Not only for being an amazing dad, but for achieving his dreams, helping me to achieve mine and building our garden room as well as our home. I could list 333 other reasons why he's a superhero and they'd all branch far beyond reading a book to his son.

Your First Birthday as a Dad

What a fitting time
To turn 33
Last year, we were a couple
Now, you're one third of a family

You're working on the third house you've built
You're the best dad to our family of three
Oh, and it might not feel like it
But it's only your third full year
Of being loved by me

You said you once thought you'd never achieve your dream
Your life wasn't going to plan
Then as soon as you weren't expecting it
The building, the providing, the family life just…
Began

It happened suddenly for both of us
Our "linear plans" got out of hand
The world has a funny way of making you think you can't
Then all at once
You can

I hope you know how proud I am
Though I don't say it enough
For building our future, working hard
And being my teammate when we both
Stop
And say "this is actually getting really tough"

Three years into your third decade
And look how far we've come
Three house builds
An engagement
Our dream house together
Welcoming our little one

And each day as we watch him
Growing wiser, growing taller
He takes our black and white world
And adds life, adds purpose, adds colour

We're building and writing the stories we'll tell him
When he's older, when he's made our hair turn grey
Like how we loved to do things differently
And maybe he'll be inspired to do the same one day

Because whilst others rushed to a timeline
Hurry! House-then-marriage-then-kids!
We rolled with it, became the people we wanted to be
And that's where the magic of our relationship lives

We've bonded through the lows
We've soared through the highs
Proven that for better or worse, we've got this
Before I've even become your wife

And when that day comes
Another landmark on our journey
It'll mean so much more than if that was our starting point
It'll cement everything we already know we can be

One day we'll reflect on this season
Your chapter 33
The one where we lived in the garden den you built
Went on an adventure - you, me and our baby

So on your 33rd birthday
It seems a fitting time
To say 333 thank-yous for all you do
You're our baby's hero
As well as mine.

WEEK 28

You can't stay a gummy bear forever

With no sleep and no needs of my own being met, this is a really tricky season. But I can do tricky; I can do impossible. Because this right here, in this snuggly blanket, is where my purpose lies, for now.

I call him Roger Red Cheeks. I'm not sure where this name came from, but it's stuck. Crimson cheeks. Sad eyes. The bottom lip curled outwards. The face that is so often wrinkled at the nose with a cheeky smile, now looks downwards. Forlorn. Without that smile, my baby seems serious beyond his years; as though he's a man with the weight of the world on his shoulders. His mournful pea head looks lost, whilst his teeny-tiny shoulders seem to slope down more than before. The reason for his irritability glints at me, in the form of a tiny white pearl in his mouth. Teething.

The soothing techniques in my mothering toolkit aren't working this time. Feeding him, patting him, carrying him around the garden to look at the plants … no, he has bigger issues to contend with now. Experiencing pain must be hard when your tiny body is only a fraction of the size of a grown up's. Whilst I wish I could take his pain away, I'm filled with gratitude that this young life knows nothing of trauma beyond teething.

Today, I declare it Mummy and baby day. I slide into my softest jumper, locate the grittiest film on Netflix and resign myself to an afternoon of sofa naps, cuddles and intermittent feeds with my son. Nobody can get to us in our humble little shed at the top of the garden – not even the loud knock of the delivery driver, which never fails to make me jump when we live in a "normal" home. The outside world busies about around us. The cars drive by for work and the trains clatter along in the distance. Our time stands still again on days like these and I love it. The motherhood meddlers and the fast-paced world are all far away from our reality as we relax in our shed amidst the bramble bushes. It's times like these that I'm at my most content. No clock-watching, no conversation-making; just pure, undiluted motherhood.

I make this sound so blissful and so easy. What a life, to cuddle on the sofa whilst the world continues to tick along. With no sleep and no needs of my own being met, this is a really tricky season. But I can do tricky; I can do impossible. Because this right here, in this snuggly blanket, is where my purpose lies, for now. I hope that when he wakes, these cuddles, naps, intermittent feeds and the teething medicine have cured his mouth full of pain. I pray that once this rising sun begins to set and the daylight turns to dark, the passage of time will have given me my jolly little baby back.

First Tooth

Eyes cast down
Bottom lip turned under
Fiery red cheeks
Tummy sounds like thunder

My baby today, looks serious
Intermittently cupping his face
His head resting on my chest
Our fingers interlaced

Wish I could take his pain away
Release him from this struggle
Medicine isn't doing the trick
And neither are my cuddles

If this bond was made of gold
We'd turn to precious treasure
If my love could cure his pain
He'd be comfortable forever

If snuggles could stop wars
We'd be cruising for world peace
If love could transcend death
I'd have my angel family with me

But there's no cure for this tricky time
We've got to ride this wave
Settling into the pain

Snuggling into the blanket den we've made

Fed up expression
Hand squeezing mine
Sleepy blinks, tear-stained face
No smiles this time

A few days later
I realise I've got my baby back
His cheeks have turned to peach again
He's bouncing on my lap

And there it is
Proving my instinct true
He smiles and a white pearl sparkles at me:
His
Very
First
Tooth.

WEEK 29

A new generation

I hope I'm successful in raising my son to know that just as smelly manure leads our roses to bloom, happiness often thrives alongside sadness.

Last week, as I watched my baby teething, I found myself wondering what life has in store for him. *Which memories will turn into his future nostalgia?* This led me to ponder how social media will affect him, and if our contemporary world of technology will hinder the magic of his childhood? Growing up, there was never a time where I got confused between what happened in my life and what happened on *The Sims* (though my mum did need to remind me to have a break from it, to eat something every now and again). Likewise, I didn't play *Snake* on my Nokia 3310, before trying to slither around in reality, slurping bits of pixelated food that made me feel like maybe I was growing so long that I bumped into myself. I didn't find myself pulling anyone's arms and legs after playing with Stretch Armstrong, never built a *LEGO* structure and mistook it for a real building. I never confused my sticky aliens in their plastic eggs for my real friends. Sadly, the boundaries of fiction and reality aren't so clear for our children.

Have we fully experienced the impact of social media on our TikTok and Instagram generation of little ones yet? I worry about my son's future exposure to this contrived existence, which makes fiction seem so real. As a '90s child, I was given a pretty solid chance at drawing a defined line underneath the make-belief world before entering back into the real one. Today's generation of babies are bound to have a tougher time doing that when they grow up, surely? Society encourages us to scroll through a sea of content that's mostly fictional, yet great at making us think it's real. What impact will this have on those growing up in this climate of online comparison?

Even following my fairly wholesome childhood, it's taken me a while to figure out that happiness and sadness live hand in hand and that sadness isn't something to be scared of. Even *my* mind was geared towards believing that sadness should be labelled as "bad" and happiness as "good". We might not have had social media, but fairytales have taught us that as women, we must sit around looking pretty and wait for a prince to sweep us off our feet so we can live happily ever after in his kingdom. Surprisingly, it's taken a while for me to figure out the path I'd like my life to take, beyond the route that fairytales told me I wanted my life to take.

I believe that fairytale-led way of thinking has made it tricky, even for our generation, to see that happiness lives alongside sadness and achievements require hard work. For our children, the fake world has taken huge leaps in serving up fictional online narratives that are hard – often impossible – to replicate. I hope I'm successful in raising my son to know that just as smelly manure leads our roses to bloom, happiness often thrives alongside sadness.

One Thing You Should Know

If there's one thing I can teach you
One thing you should know
It's that when life feels tricky
Seems you've exhausted all options
That's when inside, you grow

And your growth will take you to places
Beyond your biggest
Bravest dreams
Whilst you're striving to work it all out
The clouds will be preparing to clear
Making way for sunbeams

When life serves sour lemons
And they sincerely hit the fan
The damage might look irreparable
You might think that you can't
But I promise you
You can

Because tricky times must thrive
Before the great things grow
That's why farmers scatter fields with manure

And before we see the sun
We feel the biting frost of snow

Before we admire rainbows and flowers
We must shiver from the soaking of rain
Every great success story
Is usually preceded by knock-backs
Setbacks
Growth
Doubt
Pain

But rarely will you see those parts
Because no one ever shouts about it
The world is designed to show the highlights
The pride, the success
But never the rock-bottom bits

So whatever you're dreaming of
If the results are just not showing
Don’t be down on yourself
It means that inside
You
Are
Growing

Everything has a solution
Please never give up hope
I’ve been there before, then realised
The more I find comfort in bad times
The more the good times show

So if you learn one lesson from me
Please let it be that
And no matter where I am
Heaven or earth
I will always have your back.

WEEK 30

Avocado aeroplanes

We've gone back to basics, living the simple life in a 4 x 8 metre garden room, yet we've not once got bored. For the first time ever, I'm not craving a holiday.

We're about to try our baby with food for the first time, so this avocado has come to represent so much more than a healthy source of unsaturated fat. It's our little one's first step to independence; the first time he's not needed me for one of the key building blocks of life. After nine months of being fed by the umbilical cord and six-months-and-counting of breastfeeding, putting him in a highchair with a plate and spoon makes this segment of the journey seem less magical.

Jamie and I watch the intrigue across our son's face as we fly the food aeroplane through the air. Here comes the aeroplane: Piawwwwn. I feel like I've just swallowed my heart as he takes his first inquisitive bite and chews it slowly. It's one of many moments where I feel gratitude that I'm part of a family; that I'm part of *this* family. Who knew I could find such joy in sitting around a table in a glorified shed? We've gone back to basics, living the simple life in a 4 x 8 metre garden room, yet we've not once got bored. For the first time ever, I'm not craving a holiday. It's a good job, because we haven't been on one for a long while – other than the odd weekend away in this country.

People ask: "Where are you going on holiday this year?" and seem shocked when we say we don't have plans for one. It's not that we don't want to go away; it's just not one of our priorities right now. There's a lot going on. There was a time when I'd forever be planning my next get-away, but this adventure feels like enough for now. Holidays seem to have become a benchmark of happiness in the online world. I see it often – people elbowing each other out of the way with a saccharine string of posed photos, to prove that their holiday was better than the next person's. Should I be feeling like I'm missing out? I don't. I'd like to go away when we have a pause in this adventure. For us right now, this life experience is enough.

Once this sleep-deprived, hazy, home-building adventure ends and we're coming down from this high altitude, we'll enjoy introducing our little one to the delights of flying through the sky to discover new countries beyond the beauty of the one we live in. This time right now, in our garden room with our little one, feels precious and I've never felt so rich. So, for now, I'll leave the aeroplane noises for our weaning adventures.

Crying Over an Avocado

You're six months old and it's weaning time
It's unusual to be upset by an avocado
But I spent nine + six months growing you solely
From this clever body of mine

Now here we are, mashing up this pulp
From womb, to breast, to highchair
Now I'm blinking back tears in harmony
With your first food-filled gulp

Let's not turn this into an emotional roller-coaster
It's going in… OH
I need to turn away because
I won't admit that I'm crying over an avocado

The intrigue across your face
It puts my heart in my mouth
I saw you grow from a kidney bean
Now we have food flying
North
East
West
And south

Who would you be and what would your dad be like?
These are the scenes I used to imagine
A family of my own was a concept
I could never really fathom

I was all about independence, you see

Climbing the career ladder
Making a palace
A home, just for me

Then came the reinventions
A symptom of PMDD
Each month I'd shake up my life
How could I ever settle and have a family?

That's why this avocado makes me tearful
Because I can finally picture this day
The family scenes I never thought I'd have
But good things come to those who wait

I once craved holidays
Now I find joy in this simplicity
Just you
Your dad
An avocado aeroplane
And me.

WEEK 31

A sea of analytical eyes

I didn't know it at the time, but I went into the hospital as my own woman and left with a baby in my arms and a target on my back.

I'm at a soft play centre and see a mum with a new baby crying into the arms of her friend. I can't help but hear bits of the conversation through her staccato breaths and heavy sobs. "It feels like the world is watching me and I can't do anything right and I've not slept and don't feel like myself and I don't want help because I want to do things without being watched and all the help isn't helping anyway". This lady is a stranger, yet I feel united with her through that one, discombobulated sentence. I don't encroach upon her chat with her friend, but my mind sends her air hugs and happy-heart wishes as I head outside. My brain is whirling with the unfairness of it all. *Why do some mums find themselves under such overwhelming scrutiny, simply because they had a baby?* Since discussing this with fellow mums, I've realised that for many of us, it's often not caring for our babies that's the hardest part; it's dealing with the pressures, demands and misplaced comments from outsiders.

As new mums, we sometimes find ourselves under a looming pressure to conform to a certain way of mothering our babies. Only, as I've been discovering, there is no *one* certain way of carrying out this role perfectly. There's Pauline from Preston's certain way of doing things, Bridget from Bowness' certain way of doing things, and Sharon from Salisbury's certain way of doing things. Before these women come for me, I must point out, these names are fictional but, in my experience, the attitudes are not.

I didn't know it at the time, but I went into the hospital as my own woman and left with a baby in my arms and a target on my back. I'll be happily minding my own business on my mothering journey, guided by my instincts and then … well, well, well, if it's not someone on a full eight hours of sleep, come to ask judgement-laden questions, make irrelevant comments or roll their eyes at me. The part I find most fascinating is that before I became a mum, nobody cared if I could make a rhubarb crumble, cook a four-course meal for a busload of visitors, or fluff a pillow. Upon leaving hospital, the pressure to conduct myself in a multitude of certain ways and become a mother to people who aren't my offspring, felt heavy.

A study by baby brand Kendamil has highlighted that I'm not alone in these feelings. Kendamil's research found that 81% of mums feel they're being judged by others, whilst "37% feel it's from their mothers-in-law, 31% their own mother, 22% from school and nursery parents, and 39% even their friends".[9] We're in good company then. These stats indicate that a large portion of surveillance and judgement tends to stem, once again, from some members – certainly not all – of the older generation.

I never felt this judgement or pressure to conform to my gender's outdated stereotypes prior to motherhood. My breasts weren't a topic up for discussion, my diet was nobody's business, the way I designed my home didn't interest anyone, and it wasn't commonplace for people to force plans into my diary. Now, whether it's the way I put my son down to sleep, comments on my body, questions about my breastfeeding routine and when I'm going to stop, remarks on my cooking abilities or questions like "why doesn't he have any toys?" (It's all about clever storage, my friend), I'm under a microscope that stares into my motherhood – and my life beyond it.

When mealtimes tick around and I'm focussed on feeding my baby, I've found an expectation to also feed the ravenous stomachs of visitors who still happen to be visiting. I love welcoming friends and family over for a gathering every so often and providing food and drinks, but it seems that since becoming a mum, I'm expected to do that on a daily basis; whilst also juggling motherhood, a career, a home, and a sea of analytical eyes. It seems that becoming a mum gave birth to a requirement to display maternal attitudes to people *who are not my children*. In moments like these, I miss the freedom of doing whatever I like without being so closely monitored and called upon. For the first time in my female-liberated life, I've come up against an oppressive hand that tries to control many aspects of my world. Once again, it's a female hand I'm grappling with. That hand belongs to those who seem to have been squeezed so tightly by the grip of tradition themselves – either willingly or not – that they try to hold the younger generation with the same strength.

For all the women who have fought for female liberation, I will not let that hand win this arm wrestle. I will not let outdated expectations shape the way I mother my child or the role I play in my family. I bring plenty to the table – and that's not always a warm apple pie. I won't be cancelling my career goals, identity, and big dreams in favour of completing a traditional checklist to somebody else's expectations. I won't push mine and my son's needs aside, in favour of a constant access-all-areas pass to our lives. I'll ensure everyone who would like to spend time with our son has equal opportunity to do so – whilst remaining focussed on what works for myself and my family, rather than someone else's checklist. To be clear, I love many of the traditional roles that were historically assigned to my gender. I enjoy cleaning, homemaking, and of course, mothering my son. I've been nesting since I had my own bedroom, and I occasionally enjoy cooking. I'll never conform to tradition as an institution, though. I'll embrace the gender stereotypes that I enjoy, but they'll never become my career or the single defining feature of my identity.

During my literature studies at university, I read Margaret Atwood's *The Edible Woman* and recall feeling grateful that I'd never had to deal with the oppression experienced by the female characters in the book. I admired the novel but couldn't relate to it. Since my baby was born, I'm surprised that I can now relate to the sense of surveillance and expectation experienced by the female characters in the book. I've felt the same pressure to shed my identity, in favour of people-pleasing others. Though female autonomy has come a long way, it seems that motherhood sets us back a few steps. In *The Edible Woman*, the protagonist feels so picked apart by society that she begins to identify as food that's being consumed by the world, until she completely detaches from herself. Similarly, it feels like since becoming a mum, I've become a food item on a plate. It seems I'm there to be consumed; picked apart; for my most delicious segments to be nibbled at.

I realise these feelings are grounded in truth and not the foggy emotion of PMDD, when I see the same happening to my son. After being passed from pillar to post and metaphorically nibbled on to satiate someone's hunger pangs, he comes back to me exhausted, irritable, visibly distressed. I know I'm not the only one feeling the same suffocating pressure to forget about myself and the needs of my baby in favour of becoming a cook, a cleaner, a chauffeur, an entertainer and a personal assistant, alongside all the other roles I've fulfilled before and since becoming a mother. I also know I'm not the only mum to have felt watched and judged throughout motherhood. I've heard from so many other mums who have experienced the same.

The sad thing is, that new mums – just like discombobulated sentence lady – tend to crumble under the pressure of the surveillance, before they can build themselves back up after the birth. I wish we could stop this from happening. I wish society was geared towards supporting new mums, rather than suffocating them. If I could write a letter to my past self, there are so many things I would have told myself, to reduce the unnecessary pressure of surveillance and scrutiny from outsiders. Unfortunately, dealing with that snowstorm of unrealistic expectations seems to be yet another rite of passage in the making of a mother.

A Letter to My Past Self

Don't take on the advice of the world
Just because some have done this before
It'll become overwhelming
When you should be enjoying this magical
Natural
Journey of *yours*

They may try to fill your mind with
Their
Ideas of motherhood
Their
Pregnancy and birth scares
But remember this is your experience –
Not theirs

If visitors descend upon you and your baby
Please remember you're not a host
It's not your job to pacify others
And no, you're not "clingy"
If you prefer to hold your newborn close

Some might judge you
Maybe even friends and family members

They'll think that sly comment went under the radar
But, surprise!
A lack of support is one thing
A new mum *always* remembers

"You won't leave him for a night?
Why's that then?"
Shrug it off
Never offer an explanation
Because
You certainly don't owe one to them

You'll be judged for not shouting at your baby
Judged for not feeding him cake
Judged for "making him mardy"
People get passionate about these decisions
But
These aren't their decisions to make

When times get tricky, try to remember
One thing that will never be changed
Your baby is an extension of you
Your treasured soul
Your best, forever friend

So, when you become a mum
Be selective with the advice you listen to
You'll learn most things by yourself
And following your intuition
Is the best thing you can do.

WEEK 32

Crying over spilt milk

I'm exhausted, overstimulated, on autopilot with pre-planning, pumping and breastfeeding. And then... the milk gets spilled.

When our baby cries in the night, Jamie can walk him around for hours, or I can keep the peace by just feeding him and getting him to sleep much sooner. I say "just" feeding him; it's actually hard work. Our little one has to be in the right position, I have to be in the right position (whilst ensuring my tired eyes don't fall asleep), and once his tiny tummy is full, it's both a skill and an art to transfer him to his crib without waking him. When Jamie takes him instead, I enjoy the feeling of snuggling down and keeping my eyes closed. Luxury. It's not long though, before I start to feel guilty and the adrenaline rush of a mother in demand takes over. I know that breastfeeding will get our son to sleep faster, so each time I'm tempted to take my only opportunity to sleep, I end up feeding him anyway. I almost feel sorry for Jamie that he doesn't have functioning boobs – getting our baby to sleep requires much more walking and rocking without them.

I wake with the panic that seems to come with hearing tiny cries, making me too adrenaline-fuelled for sleep afterwards. My body is constantly fighting between the need to sleep and the need to protect my baby. It's beginning to take a toll on my health. I'm so sleep deprived that I'm not hungry anymore – I feel too tired for food and, with breastfeeding said to burn around 500 extra calories per day[10] I know I need to eat, but my sleepy state makes it seem impossible to even chew.

To ease the pressure and attempt some rest when the rare opportunity presents itself, I use long car journeys to express milk. The passenger seat and cup holder have become the main components of my milking factory. Where there once sat a Costa cup, there's now a bottle of hard-earned breast milk that will be gone in a matter of seconds, once we reach our destination. Why do I put so much patience and energy into this? It seems that even those couple of minutes of someone else feeding him, gives me a moment of mental clarity.

Once we arrive, I feel it's only polite to chat with the same energy and enthusiasm as I used to, so nobody thinks I'm rude, or that I've adopted that classic case of post-baby boring. But actually, I feel brain dead and my body feels heavy. I'm exhausted, overstimulated, on autopilot with pre-planning, pumping, and feeding. And then… the milk gets spilled.

Drained

I find it exhausting – feeding all the time
Yet what a perfect opportunity
To put my feet up and cuddle
This hungry salamander of mine

I'm finding my "new normal"
Trying to reclaim some sleep
I express milk for his dad to feed him
Catching every little leak

I express milk on long journeys
The car's cup holder is my storage
I'd like to be that woman on Facebook
Who has more milk than she knows what to do with

I express milk whilst entertaining him
I'm not spending money on that fancy pump for your bra
So I cut holes in my old lingerie
But though I had a fridge full
Even my new pumping routine doesn't spread far

Because a lot of the time, I realise
It's about comfort as well as filling his tummy
Once that marble-sized stomach is filled
He needs cuddles with his mummy

Yet that few moments of peace, makes the expressing worth it
For ten minutes he'll go with his dad
Gives me time to brush my teeth, wash my face

Have an express bath

His dad always tries to be careful
Carrying milk through the door
But with that amount of pressure
It seems
He can't hold it together anymore

Like a careful bull in a China shop
He holds the bottle steady and close
But inevitably
He has a Paddington Bear moment
And onto the floor it goes

Now it's all slow motion
My heart is in my mouth
Two hours hooked up to a milking machine
To produce the treasure that's splashing
North, east, west and south

That's when I realised that well-known phrase
Actually holds some power
Crying over spilt milk is a real thing
When it's literally
Drained you
For the last
Few
Hours.

WEEK 33

C-section pride

Do I feel like I took a shortcut or the easy way out with my C-section? Absolutely not. Nor do I feel like I missed out on the journey of birth. In fact, I feel like I saw all the landmarks and more along the way.

My baby points at everything. It's his new thing. He says "OH!?" as his tiny finger points to the trees, the flowers, the birds, the curls in his hair. This morning in the bath, his attention turned to my C-section scar; my purpley-silver trophy that marks the place where magic happened. I felt pure pride. It's funny to think that I once didn't like the thought of a C-section. To the uninitiated – and admittedly, to my pre-baby self – it may seem like the weak way out; the quick shortcut for when your female form can't fulfil one of its many functions; the loophole for those who just couldn't quite make it to the finish line; the route that you take when you're not bothered. Having now lived and breathed – yes, I breathed through every contraction – of an emergency C-section, I realise how wildly misguided my judgement was and how naive the pre-natal version of me was.

Do I feel like I took a shortcut or the easy way out with my C-section? Absolutely not. Nor do I feel like I missed out on the journey of birth. In fact, I feel like I saw all the landmarks and more along the way. Our unassisted hypnobirthing journey was calm and beautiful. Underscored by music, faux candles, and fairy lights in the midwifery-led unit, we created the most comforting atmosphere I could imagine to labour in. For me, those 50-plus hours of contraction, contraction, contraction, repeat, would have been a lot trickier without our hypnobirthing set-up. I breathed through every contraction, felt every movement and every gloriously uncomfortable, satisfyingly productive pain in our calm den at the hospital. After spending time in our birthing paradise, we got to know our midwife, Martyne, who cared for me for eleven hours whilst I dilated in the consultant-led unit. Finally, we enjoyed the magical moment of meeting our son in theatre.

As I lay with my insides splayed out on an operating table after such an intense couple of days of labour and pushing, I'm not afraid to admit that once my baby was pulled out, I felt like a warrior. Victory. I'd tried so hard to get him into the world; I'd put the work in for this, and now he was here. Pure elation. I'd never felt so awful and wonderful all at once. I'd done it and my baby was on my chest. Not for one moment, did I feel like I'd taken the "easy" way out. That was a really intense birth – but yes, it was also a C-section and I can confirm that it was by no means easy. I couldn't help but wonder if Jamie wished things had gone differently. Without getting into the emotions, the mere question brought a lump to his throat and to summarise his response, he's never felt more protective or proud as he did over those few days of labour, dilating and pushing, followed by our C-section and finally, the birth. He says he feels those few days brought us even closer together. I agree.

There's a great feeling of pride that lives alongside the memories of our birthing journey. I'm proud of Jamie for staying awake and supportive, for days, on hardly any sleep. I'm proud of how our birthing journey brought us even closer and I'm proud of my body for everything it's gone through. So, nowadays whenever someone tells me they've had an emergency C-section, my sense of empathy and respect naturally goes up a level as I can relate to what they've been through. I feel the pain of that freshly stitched skin and I ask how their scar is healing. Magic, personified.

A C-section has certainly not been the easy route. Does anybody ever have an "easy" birth? I'm not sure. However, I'm proud of how mine went. I'm glad that our caesarean has led me to the souvenir that I get to keep forever to remind me – to remind us – of the magic that happened at 7.45 on that Monday morning. I pray that this C-section scar never fades.

That Casual Little C-Section

"What's that you say?
You're a C-section mum?
Brilliant, so you just lay there?
No vaginal tears?
No pushing to be done?

You didn't have contractions?
Your bladder is still intact?
So, they numbed you and lifted the baby out
And that was simply that?"

Actually, I breathed through every contraction
Was this two births in one?
I laboured and dilated to ten centimetres
Then pushed and pushed
But even then, no baby
No, there was *more* work to be done

We didn't know I'd need a section
So we were having a "natural" birth
Then as his heartbeat became weaker
An operation was the only way
To ensure he stayed on this earth

If you've had a section – emergency or planned
Please go easy on yourself
People underestimate the toll it takes
On your physical
And mental
Health

No, you didn't get a vaginal tear
But seven layers of your body have been torn through
The world's only invasive operation
That's portrayed as "the easy route"
So here you are, getting back up
Because
Society expects you to

You've had your uterus taken out
Your fallopian tubes have seen the light of day
The doctors need to inspect them
Before they can put these magical
Organs
Away

When was the last time
You heard of someone having a major operation

Then freshly stitched, they're up and about
After just having had their body cut open?

Stop thinking you need to be superwoman
You've had seven layers of your body cut through
Your skin
Fat
Fascia layers
Muscles
Your peritoneum, too

The muscular uterus is opened up
Your little one's cosy home
And finally, the amniotic sac
Where your body has been nurturing this magic
On
Its
Own

Now here you are
I see you
Struggling to do everything at once
Because you've "only had that casual little C-section"
You're trying to be everything
To everyone

Even if I have the easiest birth next time
Even if I'm feeling fine
I won't be hosting
Or accommodating anyone
I'll be taking in what my body just did
To deliver this magical
Baby of mine.

WEEK 34

Dreaming of having my body back

Kind family and friends ask what they can do to help, but there really is nothing when you're the milk-maker and cry-tamer.

There's something to be said for the mental and physical impact of carrying a baby inside your body for nine months and giving birth, followed by the close contact of feeding, plus being on-demand to comfort your little one through each cry. It feels like my body isn't mine anymore. I'm constantly climbed over, grabbed at and fed from. After my baby's gone to bed, it's often my weary body that's struggling to stand upright as I set about the preparations for the next wholesome yet sleepy day of parenting. I find that a little organisation goes a long way in setting me up for the morning. Though Jamie is amazing at being a hands-on dad, I'm the key carer, so I'm the one who knows exactly what needs to be done for the next day when he's out at work or working on building our new home. Preparing for the following day has become a ritual. One that leaves me with only a short while to do something for myself in the evening.

I feel guilty when Jamie goes in for a well-deserved cuddle and I lose my mind. I'm not sure where this has come from, but today it's been making me feel unreasonably icky, just thinking about any further human contact. I've found a term for this, which makes me feel less alone. If you struggle with this too, Google the term "touched out" and you'll realise there are many others feeling the same way. It refers to that feeling of simply being touched all the time and getting sick of it. There's no science, stardust or impressive facts here. Just a widely experienced annoyance.

As mothers, we're often seen as the cosy comfort blanket of the family. I'm happy to be that blanket, until the eleventh hour when I realise how depleted I feel and how much I'm craving my own body back. No matter how prominent a role the father plays in a baby's life, the mum is usually the key comfort-creator in these early days. Kind family and friends ask what they can do to help, but there really is nothing when you're the milk-maker and cry-tamer. That's why I get excited for nap times. As soon as nap-o-clock ticks round, I'm all geared up to reclaim a small segment of myself for half an hour. I'll clean the garden room, have an express bath or shower and a hot drink or close my own eyes for ten minutes. Sometimes, I have grand plans, those tiny eyes close and I'm ready to spring into "mission: me!" But then I realise … I've been nap-trapped.

Nap-Trapped

Finally, we have sleep
But you didn't think this through
Your drink's going cold on the side
There's a heavy load of life admin to do
Yet your arm's stuck under this fluffy head
Those tiny arms, still cuddling you

You're getting pins and needles now
This is doing no favours for your back
You can't wait to move around a bit
That's when you realise
You've been nap-trapped

As much as you love a cuddle
You need some time for you
So, with a kiss on the head
And a stroke of the arm
It's about time you withdrew

You haven't brushed your hair yet
Your mouth still tastes of... morning
You need to get your clothes on
And when your baby wakes
Be ready to spend the day touring

Off to baby yoga, then to see his friends
Grandma's house, aunties and uncles
His social life never ends
But first you need to be presentable
Because… well,
You also need to attend

So, you peel yourself up
Slide your head off the bed
One arm, one leg
One moment...
Your other arm's gone dead

There's something about being careful
That makes you accident prone
Your gentleness leads to a wobble
Baby stirs
You've still got this
But
Welcome to the danger zone

You wiggle yourself free
Your big plans come to fruition
A peaceful bath, a hot drink
Boring jobs done on fast-forward
You're a woman on a mission

Your sleeping baby is stirring now
Your "you time" is coming to an end
A tiny cry; little arms in the air
Welcome back to the world again
My sleepy-head little friend.

WEEK 35

We will nap again

Parenthood can feel like an overwhelming culture shift, regardless of your background or social status – yet we often experience many of the same struggles through these early days.

Throwback to the coronavirus lockdown of 2020. "We will be with our friends again, we will be with our families again, we will meet again", said our late Queen, poignantly, in her official address to the nation. Whether you were rich or poor, a normal somebody or royalty, it didn't matter. Most divides were broken down when we all had lockdown in common. The Queen was right. We all mingled with our families again and went out with our friends again. We did indeed all meet again. Though I'd never venture to compare motherhood with an infectious disease – far from it – the ripple effect of lockdown itself does feel similar to new motherhood for me, in many ways. The way we all muddled through, regardless of class divides or financial status. As mums, no matter who we are or where we live, most of us are connected through these happy-sad, scared-excited, special-mundane moments of our lives.

I didn't have a baby during the lockdown, but I often think back to it now when I'm feeling overwhelmed and realise that, as new parents, we're all in the same boat. On the long nights when it seems the rest of the world is sleeping, I find comfort in thinking of mums like me. The ones overseas who speak different languages and those in my village, just a few lampposts away. The mums in their mansions and the ones tucked up in their cosy apartments, dreaming of sleep. We're all connected through our sleeplessness whilst we feed our little ones. Not forgetting the dads and the single dads. We're most definitely not alone in this.

Parenthood can feel like an overwhelming culture shift, regardless of your background or social status – yet we often experience many of the same struggles through these early days. Just like after lockdown when some of us barely knew how to socialise anymore, we will crawl out of this hazy phase and discover the different seasons beyond it. Right now, I can't imagine ever being able to sleep again without being on my constant guard. I pray for sleep, then when my baby's napping, I'm usually wide awake, protecting him. Even now, as he's snoozing away in his cot, I find myself holding my breath for a while, creating some silence in which to hopefully hear him breathing. In. Out. In. Out. I sync my breaths to his and curl towards him, ready to pounce, the moment I hear a cough or a slight struggle for breath. Each tendon tensed, each arm poised and ready for action. It's no wonder I never sleep.

I often crave a little time for myself. I pray that his cries will morph into sleeping breaths so I can curl under the covers with a book and read myself to sleep, like the old me used to. I'd get lost in Hemingway, Lawrence and Atwood's words for a while. The reality now is that sleeping is so rare for my baby, that his silence fills me with doubt and dread. I've never witnessed him struggling for breath before. I've not once seen him choke. Yet, since the day I became a mum, I've been on full alert, morning, noon and night. His dad doesn't worry like I do. I wonder if other mums panic like this, or if this is an emotional version of motherhood that's only experienced with a mind like mine?

I don't tell those who have proven unsupportive about the lack of sleep anymore because that becomes more trouble than it's worth. It's not until Jamie mentions it, kindly, in passing conversation that you see the eye rolls. That teeny slice of information becomes an ember, ready to spark judgement and make the fire of their moral high-ground blaze. Superiority mode: on. Funnily enough, nobody can help me to breastfeed my baby at 3am, yet I still get judged for not accepting offers of help.

The self-righteous comments don't make me "learn" to come around to that person's way of thinking. They don't "fix" my maternal instinct. I don't go to sleep thinking of these opinions and wake up refreshed, on a full night of sleep. Because judgemental people don't knock the maternal instinct out of me. Rather, they make me recoil into myself and push them further away. They encourage me to build a wall around myself and my baby. At some point, that same person peeps back over that wall. "Haven't seen you in a while. How're you doing? Where have you been?". On no sleep, I take no accountability for my hostility.

How can anybody, on their full eight hours of rest, assert an opinion on something so personal as someone else's motherly instincts and decisions? If there's ever a baby number two (a question I've already noticed seeping into many conversations), my wall will be higher and the water in the moat I've built around myself will flow with a stronger force. Because I know what to expect now and I know that my reaction to manipulation or judgement will not change. I won't sleep for the foreseeable. If he doesn't sleep, I'll be kept awake. If he does sleep, his silence will keep me awake. So, that's why I'm embracing this season and all the contradictions that come with it. This is the season of no sleep, no patience with the motherhood meddlers and a heart filled with worry-saturated love.

No Sleep, Repeat

My baby's no longer a newborn
Yet I still don't sleep
This boy wants to party all night
I see 1am
I see 2am
I see 3

Unsociable hours don't feel lonely now
The rest of the world unaware of the night
I've got used to this way of life
Just him and me
Busying around in the twilight

In the mornings, I'm used to rising
Fuelled only by love
I find energy in fresh air
In nature
Necessity
At the bottom of a coffee cup

I've heard others call the doctor
"Please just give my baby something"
This little life doesn't need medication
Just endless cuddles
And feeds
And loving

There wasn't a clock in my womb
It's taking a while to adjust
My baby craves comfort at hours
That are normal for him
Though unsociable for us

Sometimes I get frustrated
This is all too much
But I need patience
To know it won't last forever
And to always believe in hugs before drugs

He doesn't always need feeding
It's the security he's after
Feeding him is the simplest way
To welcome the return of peace
Sleeping breaths
And early morning laughter

Hand holding isn't enough
He needs comfort at its best
Tiny body encased in mine
Legs dangling over the side
Pummelling at my chest

I need to embrace this
One day he won't wake for a cuddle and bum pat
I won't hold his sweet dough body
Or feel his tiny bottom in his babygrow
Nothing can ever beat that

The only way he'll sleep sometimes
Is to keep him in our bed for the rest of the night
So I don't sleep myself
Obsessing over watching him
Checking he's alright

No Sleep, Repeat

"You'll never get any sleep", they say
"You're making a rod for your own back"
I'll carry that rod with pride because
I'm 100% okay with that.

WEEK 36

Postnatal depletion

If we allow women one month or more of pure, uninterrupted rest and bonding with their babies, would they be in a better place mentally and physically, to continue with the rest of their motherhood journeys? I believe so.

Evidently, I've lost an "are-you-okay?" amount of weight. I'm gaunt, run-down, often poorly, and as mentioned last week, I hardly sleep. Somehow, I haven't slept for longer than a four-hour stretch for over a year. Even before I had my baby, pregnancy and hyperemesis did *not* lend themselves to recuperation. Though grateful for the "you're doing amazing"s and "you look great"s, I sometimes feel like a piece of roadkill that would have survived if someone rescued it. I don't need rescuing by someone telling me to pump milk and hand my baby over for the day. I don't need rescuing through plans being forced into my diary or endless questions and photo requests spilling into my phone. "Let me come and help", followed by me hosting that person instead of napping during my baby's naps, doesn't help. Having people visiting my baby often, under the disguise of help, then handing him back for nappy changes whilst I'm also playing waitress to that visitor (and praying that this coffee will be their last before they leave), is not helpful.

For me, help is having any demands on my time, completely expelled. If someone is coming to visit, it's helpful when they muck in with the unpopular jobs. Help is clearing away the baby paraphernalia that everyone keeps tripping over. Help is a loved one patting my baby's bum and carrying him around the living room whilst I rest my weary body on the sofa, unjudged. Instead, I've found that for a large part of this year, I've been badgered with requests for things that I've made it clear I'm not comfortable with – like taking him for a day out when I know full well, my baby would not be comfortable with this. And neither would I. Plus, the breastfeeding situation and if I hear the phrase "pump then!" one more time...

As well as the unwanted outside pressure, I do feel that if I'd have stopped the self-inflicted "need" to host everyone else just one day after giving birth and having a major operation, I'd have healed now that we're 36 weeks into parenthood. Instead, I put all these pressures on myself and it's made me quite unwell. My body and brain don't feel as though they've had time to heal from pregnancy, let alone the birth, so I've gone right back to basics and I'm finding the simplest things a struggle – particularly when I'm hosting as though I'm not also trying to keep another life alive with my own exhausted body.

I'm not blaming anyone else for my exhaustion. I should have asserted my boundaries from the beginning. Only, I was new to motherhood, so I didn't know there would be boundaries that needed to be asserted. Nor did I know I was losing an identity that would need to be re-discovered. I was simply too naïve, exhausted and excited to think about myself and how I needed to be on as top form as possible for my boy. I'm beginning to wonder if this is everyone's experience of motherhood, or just mine? Though happy, fulfilled and grateful, I'm seriously running on empty. I feel hypervigilant, as though my brain is in an always-alert state of protection. I'm like a happy-poorly-exhausted robot that's been switched to turbo mode, using batteries that should've been replaced a year ago. Yet here I am, squeezing the dregs out of the old Duracells because I have no time to replace them.

My sleepy brain is finding it difficult to hold conversations, or to remember even the simplest things. Mothering my baby is easy in many ways – I'm guided by my instincts. It's the outside pressures of modern motherhood like diary management and hosting that feel tricky. It turns out that this set of symptoms is yet another widely experienced yet lesser-discussed part of motherhood. It's called "postnatal depletion" – a term coined by family practitioner, Dr. Oscar Serrallach. He names fatigue and exhaustion, feeling tired on waking, falling asleep unintentionally, loss of self-esteem, overwhelm and brain fog amidst the symptoms. These usually derive from lack of rest, poor nutrition and generally taking care of our babies so much that we neglect ourselves. This decline in our own health and wellbeing begins before our babies even arrive.

The brain of a pregnant woman undergoes a "software upgrade", as Serrellach defines it, which ignites the motherly instinct we need to care for our little ones. "This is not discussed or respected enough in our society, and I feel mothers need much support and acknowledgement for this new phase of life"[11] says Serrellach. In non-scientific terms, the brain's so-called software upgrade is what drives us to feed those baby-bird mouths, snuggle them in a blanket when they're cold, or pick them up when they cry. It's what makes us put their needs before our own. "This hyper vigilance is obviously vital for the survival of the child but if living in an unsupportive society, it can lead to sleep problems, self-doubt, and insecurity", says Serrellach.

I'm cocooned in a supportive circle with those closest to me, though I do believe that our society as a whole isn't geared towards caring for postpartum women. I've highlighted the lack of care throughout this book, in terms of judgemental comments and the outdated gender stereotypes often assigned to modern mothers. Layer this upon not sleeping or eating properly, add a lack of key vitamins that Serrellach notes often remain unreplenished after birth and *of course* we're mentally and physically depleted. There's simply no time for recovery – yet imagine how parents and their babies could flourish, if they were given that time?

Just as I'm wondering what kind of support I feel myself and other mums would benefit from, I read about the Chinese custom of "zuo yue zi"'. It translates to "sitting the month" and is a long-time tradition involving new mums staying at home for one month or longer after giving birth. This helps them to emotionally, nutritionally and physically replenish every facet of their bodies and souls before they continue healthily into motherhood. No onslaught of visitors, no ferrying our new little loves around to satiate everyone's desire to see them – just pure, wholesome recuperation.

Whilst some of the practices involved in this tradition aren't up my street – eating pigs' feet for example – I'm firmly on-board with the idea behind it. The tradition encourages new mums to rest and relax, replenish their nutrient stores and make the most of dedicated assistance with any potential feeding glitches or the other issues that can feel tricky to begin with. It also aims to discourage new mums from doing housework, lifting heavy objects or hosting family and friends in favour of recovering.

Of course, whilst we all find it easy to ask someone close to us to hold our baby whilst we make them a drink, it sometimes becomes awkward or overly familiar to request care that relates to ourselves. I'd feel uncomfortable asking a friend or family member to cook my tea, care for my baby next to me whilst I sleep or apply a compress to my scar. That's where, in Chinese tradition, the "pui yuet", or postnatal confinement nanny comes in. This is the person who makes sure all of the above is carried out seamlessly. The pui yuet ensures the new mum is consuming the right nutrients, gaining the right amount of rest and not spending the baby's nap times worrying, tidying, or in my case, shining champagne glasses and cleaning the skirting boards. Clearly my nesting mode will never be tamed.

All the times my postpartum mind has dreamed of being *properly* looked after, the tradition of zuo yue zi loosely defines the kind of care my instincts have been calling for. It's not about having someone over to cuddle my baby whilst I host them. It's not about having a friend or family member whisk my son away whilst I lie awake on the bed crying for him. It's not about catering to the demands of family members who crave alone time with my son. It's about me, as a new mother, being given the time, grace and space to heal, without the wider pressures of needing to host and play mother to everyone. It's about prioritising the recovery of myself to make sure my son has a healthy, happy mum.

Whilst I wouldn't change a thing about how I look after my baby in these early days, I would change most things about how I look after *myself* if I ever experience new motherhood again. I've spoken to Jamie about this and we've both agreed that naturally, in the excitement and joy of our baby bubble, my healing needs weren't always met. Whilst Jamie's support was amazing, I would have benefited from a higher, more professional level of understanding in terms of nutrition and rest requirements. The scar healing and breastfeeding advice was second to none and I honestly couldn't have asked for more from our already overstretched NHS.

I'm impressed by our National Health Service's caring capabilities. There wasn't a day that went by where I felt unsupported. In the newborn haze, it seemed like the moment I had pain during breastfeeding, a lactation consultant arrived. Whenever I had a question about my son's needs, Trish the Health Visitor was here. Trish even displayed zuo yue zi-like care when she took my baby's GP forms to the surgery and wrote me a nutrient-packed shopping list. She became a fleeting friend who I'll never forget. The same with Martyne, our midwife, whose care extended far beyond her role. Expecting any more from our highly skilled, overworked and under-funded NHS would be absurd.

I do believe though, that postpartum care needs to extend beyond the first day or two after giving birth, whether that care comes from a willing friend or family member, a doula, or simply a higher level of understanding from society as a whole, on how to care for new mums. If we allow women one month or more of pure, uninterrupted rest and bonding with their babies, would they be in a better place mentally and physically, to continue with the rest of their motherhood journeys? I believe so.

At present, doula services and other extended care options are often financially unobtainable for many. Yet, in the words of Dr. Serrallach, in most cases "as soon as a baby is born, the whole focus goes to the baby. There's very little focus on the mother. The mother disappears into the shadows of her role". If we could educate society on the needs of postpartum women, rather than putting pressure on them, I believe this would be a huge step forward in avoiding postnatal depletion. The way society is currently wired to place more demands on the shoulders of postpartum women is not fair or healthy.

When I reflect on my very early days of new motherhood, I realise I minimised mine and my family's needs in favour of ticking all the boxes that society laid-out for me. I was like a tired, skinny hamster that was sweating its balls off to reach its destination, unaware that the journey would never reach its end. Though I'll never relive those early days as a brand new, first-time mum, if we ever have another baby in the distant future, I'll make sure there are plans in place that have my recovery and our baby's needs at the front and centre. I'll remember those who dropped everything to help, and those who demanded more of me and let their expectations run wild when I needed nothing but love, support and time with my baby. Most of all, I'll be taking inspiration from the zuo yue zi customs to empower myself with the opportunity of rebuilding and thriving as a new mum.

You Do Know That, Don't You?

"Mum"
You might have a new name
But you still have needs, too
It's normal to miss yourself
You do know that, don't you?

You're entitled to reject visitors
Those who turn up
Unannounced at your door
You're allowed alone time with your family
That's what these postpartum days are for

A stereotype made by society
How did you end up mothering everyone?
Fresh out of hospital
Barely functioning
Already, the care for you
Is over and done

So you spread yourself thin
For an expectant society
That you never once knew
That came as a surprise to me
I imagine it came as a surprise to you

You might have new eyes to wipe
But yours are still allowed to cry, too
Your needs are *so* important
You do know that, don't you?

I know there's rarely time, though
You're ticking off the new roles assigned to you
The cleaner, wardrobe stylist, bum-changing operative
The host, the ouchy-kisser
The masseuse

Your "mum" label comes with pressure
To blend yourself into all the cracks
Once everyone is happy
The house is tidy
The tummies are full
No matter what the order
You'll often come last

Last to have breakfast
Last to get dressed
Last to shower
The last to find a moment to say
"If there's time – *please* just half an hour?"

Thirty minutes to re-discover your old self
Half an hour to do everything you once did
Except now you're doing it on fast-forward
Whilst exhausted
Sore
Depleted

Yet, you continue this fast pace
Only now perhaps a little more put together
You'll continue marching on with a sheen to your hair
Maybe freshly-shaved legs
This pace won't last forever

It's okay to turn your phone off
To put all those messages on mute
Those who love you will offer a float
For this pressured tide
You're swimming through

It feels like you don't exist sometimes
None of your needs are being met
You're entitled to food, drink, love and happiness
I just needed to remind you
Because
Being a mum
That's easy to forget.

WEEK 37

A sister like mine

I couldn't think of a more effective support strategy – it feels like she's gone to university and completed a degree in the Chinese custom of zuo yue zi that I explored last week.

Some events in life highlight a divide in society. For example, during big sales in retail, some queue patiently; others push to the front and fight over televisions. During lockdown, some made care packages and delivered them to the vulnerable; others fought over toilet roll. I noticed a similar divide in my own world. My supportive friends and family have elegantly raised their hands to help, whilst others have either disappeared from my life completely, or spent this past year making it known that they'd like our baby to fit into their life, around their demands and schedules – and not the other way around. It's unhealthy to feel shackled by other people's expectations. As parents, we have enough on our plates, so I have my blinkers on and I'm doing things my way.

Prior to parenthood, I thought I was wonderful at caring for new families. In many ways, I was. I'd be open to travelling to them, so they didn't need to uproot all their baby paraphernalia along with their baby's routine. Before I arrived, I'd stop at the shop and ask if they needed anything. I'd happily work to their routine and make my own drinks when I arrived. Even so, my sister blows my caring qualities out of the water. She cares for us in a way I didn't know existed. Amidst those who scramble to see my baby on their own schedules, she takes an elegant step back, then goes one step further than I would ever expect, in looking after me. She treats me as the main event – never the encore. She doesn't grab my baby and cuddle him all the way to the car. Instead, she folds the pram down and lifts its bulky frame into her boot, then drives us off on adventures. When we get home, she heads straight indoors and makes us both a cup of tea. Once everyone's settled, *that's* when she scoops her nephew up and plays all the fun aunty games that she does so well. Her love is unfiltered, gentle, and selfless.

I'll never lose sight of how lucky I am to have a sister like mine. I'm not sure where she learned it, but she has this innate ability to care for my baby by caring for me first. I couldn't think of a more effective support strategy – it feels like she's gone to university and completed a degree in the Chinese custom of zuo yue zi that I explored last week. She'll unload the dishwasher, change a nappy, or bring me the old, familiar comfort blanket I know and love in the form of a sweetly scented *Buzzy Bee Bakery* box. That humble brown cardboard box sits on the side and a hint of my old self winks back at me. My sister doesn't ask lots of questions or force me to make decisions that my foggy brain doesn't know the simple answer to. Instead, she sets about cleaning the counter tops, and making us drinks and snacks. She hosts me in my own home and has done since my baby was born. I've never expected this level of care for us, but I appreciate it beyond measure.

Last month, I was burning myself out whilst catering to everyone else's needs again. Being a recovering people-pleaser takes time. In the process, it sometimes feels like raising my baby and looking after my family leaves my sense of self scattered across the floor in tiny jigsaw pieces that need to be arranged into a logical order and put back together again. Sometimes I manage it; others, I'm dealing with a 2000-piecer and my tired eyes don't stand a chance. Then, just as everything is feeling like a riddle that will never be solved, my favourite puzzle-decoder walks through the door, in the familiar shape of my sister. I couldn't do motherhood half as well without her.

Jigsaw Pieces

Thank you for loving us
In the relentless way that you do

As these jigsaw pieces litter the floor
You gather the ones that make up him

Yet with haste, you scramble to find
The pieces that are shaped like me, too

The definition of building me up
Adding marbles to my empty cup

No judgement, no eye rolls
No pushing me aside, no sarcasm

Just a human looking at two more humans
And filling our world with love

You're the fresh air on my stagnant days
The gentle breeze that flutters through

When it feels I don't know who I am anymore
You piece me back together

You're there for us
And us for you

No fuss, no push, no shove
No "*I* love him the most"

Easing him into the world
Re-introducing it to me

And whilst some fight to love and hug him
Your gentle wings encompass us both

Just as I'm ready to box-up my jigsaw
Piece myself back together another time

You see I've added many of the pieces
So you place the tricky ones in the middle

The detailed parts, like his corkscrew curls
These hazy, love-blind eyes of mine

How did you learn how this jigsaw fits together?
That loving him, involves loving me

That behind the scenes of this sweet baby

There's a tired human who needs extra hands

And appreciates being scooped up
Taken on adventures as our wonderful three

I hope you know how grateful I am
And one day, he'll show his gratitude, too

When he can express how he's forever felt
Your warmth, your care, your love

One day he'll show you our favourite jigsaw
And you'll see that the centre piece
Is you.

WEEK 38

Dancing with dark thoughts

I hope I've done a good enough job of leaving an indelible mark on his heart throughout his early years. I hope that wherever I am, in life or death, he will forever feel the comfort and stability that I've swaddled him in since birth.

My reinventions remind me of *Stars in Their Eyes*. In my head, I've twirled through that sparkle-spangled curtain showcasing many different guises, in such short periods of time. Yesterday, I was straight-thinking, emotion-free and practical but tonight ladies and gentlemen, in my detailed brain that picks apart every facet of life, we have: death. My mind has been consumed by detailed thoughts of what will happen if I pass away before my baby has grown up. I've always accepted it'll happen one day, yet the notion of death has never phased me like this before. Having a baby has shone a light on my mortality; the prospect of death just got real. If I go too soon, who will share the details of my baby's early days with him? Of course, we have photos and his dad and other family members and friends could tell him about his early life from their perspective, but I'm the only person who has been by his side for 24 hours, seven days a week for the full duration of his life so far. I am *his* person.

When he hurts himself, *I'm* the person he reaches for. When he's hungry, he rummages at my chest. When I show him how hard his daddy is working on our new home at the other side of the garden, it's me he looks back at and smiles with the pride that we share. My mind is home to all his precious early memories and there's nobody else in this world who can one day share the random little "I remember when…"s with him. No one else would have carried him as precious cargo throughout pregnancy, felt him kick, or listened to his heartbeat from inside their own tummy. So, can anyone else ever love him quite so deeply as I do? No one else carries the cells he left behind when he was growing in my tummy. If you're not familiar, it's called foetal microchimerism and I'll write more about this fascinating and comforting science next week. My thought for this week though, is that a part of him is me and a part of me is him, so if I go too soon, I'd leave a part of me on earth, and fly a part of my son around whatever or wherever it is that lives – or not – beyond life.

If I went too soon, my place at the table would be empty for a while and no doubt the sound of my voice would still echo through the kitchen; my blonde hairs would still get stuck to everyone's clothes and my clothes would still hang next to my son's in the wardrobe for a while. Yet, as the days morph into weeks, months, and years, signs of my physical presence would slip further away. I hope I've done a good enough job of leaving an indelible mark on his heart throughout his early years. I hope that wherever I am, in life or death, he will forever feel the comfort and stability that I've swaddled him in since birth.

Considering everything we go through on the journey to and through motherhood, I feel like parents should be blessed with immortal superpowers, if only for that short period of time when our babies depend on us for everything. The thought of him looking for me and me not being there, breaks my heart. I need to take care of my health, my body, and my mind to give me the best chance of being here for him for as long as possible. Right now, I have a life depending on me, as well as more milestones to celebrate, and his early memories to share with him around the dining table when he grows up. Yet, sadly that's not always how it works out. I'll write him a poem; in case I ever do fly away before he's a grown man and my hands never do get to hold his on the earth-side of life again.

If I Were to Fly Away

If I were to fly away
An eternal holiday from earth

Please know our souls are entwined forever
They have been since your birth

Our bond cannot be broken
This love cannot be undone

Though our umbilical cord is invisible now
Our hearts will still be one

Science says your blood cells
Passed through my placenta

They'll permeate my tissues and organs
For the best part of forever

So if I go to soon, the "other" world will feel the force
Of our bond that's been eternal since your birth

I'll take care of that in Heaven
It'll live on through you on earth

When you need someone on your team
Who will fight for you from the start

Remember I may be flying through the stars
But my support is engraved into your heart

If I were to fly away
If my hands could no longer hold yours

I'll be watching proudly and pointing you out
To your great-grandma from above

Because this pride cannot be described
Our connection reaches beyond life, beyond measure

When my body is absorbed by the earth
Our bond becomes invisible treasure

I hope your baby heart would forever benefit
From all the love I gave

Your love is etched into my body
The pride I have for this C-section scar

Will twirl and dance

Upon my grave

I'll take a sprinkle of this friendship you've given
The love that's written across your face

I'll soar it up to the stars
Fly it around all the planets in space

So whenever it feels like you can't
Trust me that you can

I'll be casting special powers down
Turning you into superman

It would break my heavenly heart to see your tears
And be unable to wipe your eyes

My shadow won't walk by yours anymore
Because it'll cast straight up to the sky

So if you find yourself missing me
In spring, look up at that magnolia tree

I am the dancing petals
That I used to admire with my morning tea

I am the softness and safety at night
When you're wrapped up in your quilt

I'm the lyrics that make you smile
The warmth in the house that Dad built

It's my biggest fear
If the world subtracted one from our three

But whatever the season, look in the mirror

You got those almond eyes from me

If I go too soon
Remember I'm still with you

I'm still holding your hand
I'm just holding it
From somewhere new.

WEEK 39

Fascinated by foetal microchimerism

Did you know that during early pregnancy, a low level of the baby's cells cross the placenta and migrate into the mother's blood?

Last week's detailed thoughts have got me appreciating every miniscule part of life and, on a deeper level than before, treasuring the scientific art of what my body did to grow and birth our baby. Did you know that during early pregnancy, a low level of the baby's cells cross the placenta and migrate into the mother's blood? These cells can stay there for decades or even forever, after pregnancy – whether the baby is miscarried or born – and become part of our own tissues. It's called foetal microchimerism.[12] Our babies literally become part of us; when they're in our tummies but also when they're here in the outside world beside us.

I love the idea of always carrying part of my son with me, even once he's a grown man. I can't imagine him as a grownup – it seems way too far in the future to picture it clearly, but if there's one thing I've been reminded over and over, it's that this time "will go so fast". It's true. I wish people would stop with the repetition, but it's true. I often rub my pregnant stomach and then realise I'm not pregnant anymore. That "baby kick" was just a tummy grumble, this time. Where did those pregnancy days slip off to? Having a human in my tummy feels like a second ago. The days when he was a newborn lying across my arm like a koala hugging a branch feels like a whole different era of my life.

I once heard someone say that nothing ever stays exactly the same for longer than three months, so if you're worrying about something, don't; if you're enjoying something, appreciate it. This truth has become particularly poignant throughout motherhood. Every few weeks – and certainly every three months – he's like a different baby to the one he was before, whether that's evident in his physical appearance, or his brain development. I flick back through photos and am reminded of all his different phases, highlighting the speed of time. When people say to make the most of every second, it sounds like a throw-away statement. Yet, if you dig a little deeper, the tangible meaning behind that phrase is "practice mindfulness". I agree. Mindfulness is an integral part of this new-motherhood journey. I make sure my days are punctuated with moments to take it all in. Appreciating the good, the bad, and the mundane, I'm grateful for having everything exactly the way it is right now.

The Right Way Around

Thank you
Little one
For bringing me into the present
Making me appreciate the small things
Teaching me life's most profound lessons

I relish every second because time moves too fast
From your tiny size
To the family we have alive
What we have now
Isn't designed to last

But life's too short for torturous thoughts and overthinking
I already miss you in my tummy
Listening to your heartbeat
Feeling you kicking

The miracle of having a baby
I'll never take it for granted
I remember the scans, the excitement, the magic
When motherhood often feels frantic

Thank you, little one
For highlighting the best bits of life
By laughing your head off at other babies crawling
Finding satisfaction in a pepper slice

As adults, we guzzle food
Barely even noticing
And here you are taking in
The taste, the texture

The... everything

All these years later
I finally look after myself
Because I can't have you
There is no "us"
If I've not got my health

So thank you little one
For turning my life upside down
And revealing that all along
This was actually
The right way around.

WEEK 40

Adventure under the stars

Where would I style the baby shoes he won't wear until he's one, the toy train that's for 3+ year-olds and the shelf brimming with magical books that he won't be able to read yet?

A few days after we found out I was pregnant, we discussed the idea of a nursery. Jamie highlighted that there was perhaps not much point in creating a nursery when we were soon to be moving house. I sobbed and sobbed for hours. It was the first time we both noticed how much I was bursting to the brim with pregnancy hormones. I had this deep sense of guilt, as though I was letting my unborn baby down. How could I know he was coming into the world and not prepare a special space, just for him? Where would I style the baby shoes he won't wear until he's one, the toy train that's for 3+ year-olds and the shelf brimming with magical books that he won't be able to read yet?

A family member pointed out that he's a foetus and has no idea now that he doesn't have a nursery – nor will he when he's born, nor will he when he's one. Panic over. I can honestly say that if we had a nursery, our baby wouldn't have used it once. I'm actually finding the compact living arrangements of our garden room to be handy for bringing up a little one. Anything I've lost, can only turn up in a metre or two's time and there's no running up and down the stairs or searching through different rooms as I used to before. Maybe fancy shed life is the way forward? I wouldn't recommend it in a heatwave, though.

It's a scorching July day and the garden room is so hot that we're off on yet another adventure. This time, we're spending our first night in our new home. It's not finished yet – nowhere near. We have coverings on the dusty floor in the front room and Jamie has created a grown-up den for us to sleep in. We have fairy lights, a laptop to watch a film on, and snacks. I've dressed our mattress in fresh, breezy cotton sheets and brought all our cushions with us from the garden room. Our baby is snoozing away in his travel cot next to us. We had the best rest for a long time in our blissfully cold reno project front room. This experience is highlighting the important things in life. A Pinterest-perfect nursery will be nice one day, but it will never provide a family bonding experience like this one. I wouldn’t change adventures like this for the world.

Camping in the Front Room

Through these makeshift curtains
We can see the stars
Camping in our renovation living room
Watching films on a laptop
Underscored by the nighttime hum
Of lorries and cars

This is the most haphazard living set up
Either of us have seen
But material things don't matter
I don't need a wardrobe
Or a fancy nursery
Not when I have my team

We've spent four months in a garden room
Our luxuries have been put on pause
But the boil-a-baths will be worth it
When we permanently move
Into the home
We've been working towards

Because imagine the ease of parenthood
When we've been through all we're going through now
When bath time is as simple
As turning a tap
Then reaching into an organised cupboard
For warm fluffy towels

When we have time to relax
Spend weekends as a family of three
Doing the homely things we’ve dreamed of
Chatting about our days around the dining table

Family baths
Decorating the Christmas tree

But as we flee the garden room to escape the heatwave
And camp out in this blissfully cold room together
I realise those luxuries could never come back
I know I can still find happiness
In being part of this family
Forever

So here we are on a mattress
Set down on a dusty floor
Laughing in the dark with no electric
Realising these are special memories
These are the moments
We live for

Baby asleep in his travel cot next to us
A blanket draped to block the light
My face aches from smiling
As I find joy in the simple things:
Our baby by our side
And a kiss goodnight.

WEEK 41

Social suffocation and setting boundaries

I declare myself out of the never-ending circle of planning, organising, arranging, texting, checking-in. I've officially checked out. Over and out.

My freedom continues to be violated – not by my baby; but by those who continue to put demands on our time on a daily basis, combined with me forgetting to set my boundaries because not only have I set them a million times over, I'd simply like to focus on this most precious little person in front of me during these precious early days of motherhood. Is that too much to ask? If it's not daily meetups, it's hourly texts. I understand, he's the star of the show and I'm trying my best to tick off this round-robin of plans and to-dos and meet-ups, for the portfolio of people in his life who would like to see him. But it sometimes feels like my best is never good enough.

I realise that a lot of the time, when I could be practising that classic "nap when he naps" advice, enjoying the things I love to do as part of maintaining my sense of "me", or even simply sitting and breathing, I'm actually spending that time trying to thrive in my unexpected and new-found admin role of managing expectations. Replying to the round-robin of texts: "When can I see him?" "And me, and me, and me? When's he free?" is exhausting. I'm drowning under the pressure of being a modern mum in a world that expects us to thrive with independence, whilst conforming to traditional stereotypes.

If others feel they don't see him enough now, what will happen when we go back to being a "normal" family – when we go on holidays and road trips and long weekends away? This week has felt tricky, so I confided in Jamie about this, and found his response both profound and inspiring: "It does feel like there's more expected of us since having a baby", he says, "It does feel like we need to be everything to everyone. I don't worry about it, though, because if I'm busy for multiple weekends in a row and others don't want to fit in with that, it's not my problem. If people feel upset because they haven't seen him for their definition of "a while" but we're busy as a family, not our problem. Stop making other peoples' problems, your problem. We are allowed our own life, you know". What a simple yet refreshing viewpoint. From this day forward, I vow to follow his lead. I declare myself out of the never-ending circle of planning, organising, arranging, texting, checking-in. I've officially checked out. Over and out.

Thank You, but No

Thank you for your opinion
I'm sure you don't mean any harm
But I'm struggling on no sleep
Postpartum hair loss and eye bags
Are knocking my confidence
I'm trying so hard to stay calm

Thank you for your opinion
But please do keep it to yourself
I need to focus on me and my baby
Not ticking boxes
Or jumping through these hoops
Set by everybody else

Thank you for your opinion
But it's really getting under my skin
He's only recently been born
And already
I'm judged for how I feed him
For the clothes I'm dressing him in

I carried my baby for nine months
I'll forever wear the C-section scar
When I need alone time
I'm entitled to keep him as
"Mine"
Not "ours"

Our decision to have a baby

Doesn't mean we force-share our life
With anybody else
Sometimes me and my family
Crave a little time to ourselves

And no longer will I apologise
For not wanting to see you today
When I tell you I've not slept
I'm not feeling sociable
That's not a cry for help because
I wouldn't have it
Any
Other
Way.

WEEK 42

Shed life at its finest

When I think back to growing up, my most wholesome memories – even amidst the holidays and magical days out – involved the adventures close to home.

It's the basic things that keep our little ones content in these early days. "I bet my baby wishes he was ferried around in the newer version of our car, and that the footprints of his first steps will leave the words 'Balenciaga' in the sand. I bet his babyhood would be complete if our home had a bigger square footage and an extra bedroom", said nobody in the history of parenthood ever. Naturally, there have been days in the garden room where I've wished we lived in a house; where I've wondered if we've bitten off more than we can chew or if parenthood would be easier if we were doing it the "normal" non-shed way. Yet, when I look at my baby, I realise how irrelevant this is to him. In fact, he's enjoying the adventure of our shed life – and I'm enjoying it with him.

I see his excitement in the way he holds his hands out to swoosh through the flowers and shrubs when I carry him through the garden to go out or come home. I note it in the way he pulls himself up on the headboard in the morning, sticks his head through the curtains and watches the birds and rabbits playing in the wild undergrowth behind our temporary home. He's not bothered about any of the things I worry he is missing out on. In fact, it's quite the opposite. He's thriving amidst the adventure. It's the best sensory experience ever.

When I think back to growing up, my most wholesome memories – even amidst the holidays and magical days out – involved the adventures close to home. Like when my mum gave my sister and I a budget to buy anything we wanted from a charity shop as she taught us the value of money. Or going shopping for new school shoes in the holidays. Granted, the foot measuring was tedious but I loved sitting together for a drink and a snack in a cosy café to break up the day. I also enjoyed helping my mum out around the house, learning to do the bits that I knew took a weight off her shoulders. I never craved a holiday. I always felt content simply being surrounded by the love of my family, even in the most mundane moments. I didn't care about what our house or car looked like and I didn't keep a tally of trips abroad. I believe our family bond grew stronger during the most mundane moments of everyday life.

Likewise, my baby doesn't care whether we live in a palace or a shed – everything's an adventure to him. In fact, I wonder if in some way, this shed life has strengthened my bond with him more than if we chose the easy route. I believe it has. In him, I see my baby, my best friend, wingman and adventure partner. He'll probably never know it, but he's helped me through some of my toughest times. We've adapted to life in the garden room together. We grow together. We do everything together at the moment. No matter what happens in the future and where his life journey takes him, I'll forever be grateful to have a best friend like him.

A Best Friend Like You

He's my faithful little friend
My metric that proves love has no end
My most meaningful times
My unfinished sentences
My " – oh, never mind"
My reason to stand tall and stay strong
My "okay, if you must steal him away but –
Please not for long"
My "doesn't time fly?"
My happiest tears
My heartiest cries
My alarm clock
My stopwatch
My funny little guy

My little tinker who insists on nestling in bed between us
My "who knew love could be laborious?"
My smile on my face
Even when my world's turned grey
My "there's so much to do but…
… let's leave that for another day"
My muse; my fascination

My twists, my turns
My inspiration
My “one day I’ll get my sleep back”
My "oh, I didn't expect that"
My fairytale that came true
My "how did I grow
A best friend like you?”

WEEK 43

"Let's pretend we have our sh*t together!"

They don't see the time we spend calming their cries, or how we put every element of our own lives on the back burner forevermore. You can guarantee they feel it, though.

Motherhood at the moment, feels like a sequence of putting out metaphorical fires. Today, I forgot to put the child lock on the under-sink cupboard. Whilst I was cleaning the remnants of a nappy explosion, my baby had helped himself to a bottle of washing-up liquid and created a slip-and-slide across the floor. Whilst I was cleaning that up, he tipped his dad's paperwork across the room. Some days, it feels like I'm putting out one fire and my baby is setting off another three. I happily dart around, clearing a trail of destruction from the one I love most whilst playing, learning, and having fun with him. These days are tiring, yes, but they're also full of wholesome memories and future nostalgia. Still, there comes a point in our day when I like to create a sense of calm for us all. Slowing the pace, tidying everything away and doing something mindful with my baby has become a much-needed punctuation mark in our routine.

I love the animated moments when my baby is wreaking havoc around the house. They're like a clumsy scene from *Mr Bean* or *Paddington Bear*; my life wouldn't be the same without them now. Still, I appreciate the balance provided by the calmer times. For me, faking serenity is a sure-fire way to stop a manic-mum day in its tracks. It's become a half-past-four-ish ritual. Fabricating a feeling of calm through an acoustic playlist and a tidy home can bring about a real sense of peace. It's date night and I'm telling Jamie about this routine that he'd never otherwise know about, because it all happens before he gets home from work. We agree that this isn't only a way to mark the end of the most full-on part of mine and our baby's day; it's a relationship-preservation technique. It sets our family up for a relaxed, wholesome evening. Jamie went on to reveal his own fatherhood version of this technique. When he's driving home from work, tired, he listens to dance music at full-blast, and it brings him back to life again. "It helps me to leave my day at work and come home to you both in a good mood", he says. Faking a feeling really can make the feeling happen all by itself.

I learned that life hack from my mum. "Quick, let's tidy up fast", she said, "Let's pretend we have our sh*t together!" I remember her saying this in 2016. It was after we'd spent a few days at our family home, grieving the passing of my grandma. My stepdad was on his way home, hence the statement, and my mum wanted to ensure we were pausing our grieving time with a breath of fresh reality and showing that we were coping. Once we were all tidy, present and correct, we all agreed to feeling somewhat better. I love that idea. Perhaps that outlook plays a role in my love for tidy, homely interiors. Throughout adulthood, having my home in order is, for me, synonymous with having my life together. I like giving myself time to be jumbled and disorderly before re-adopting the structure that makes me feel grounded again. This is a concept I've carried into motherhood.

I think about my mum and how she went through later motherhood as an independent homeowner, business owner and parent. Now that I'm a mum myself, my appreciation for her has grown exponentially. I've always known her as I do now – mine and my sister's built-in bestie, my main confidante, the one I turn to when life goes south. I never ventured to imagine the journey she must have been on before us, or with us – until I had a baby of my own. I've never thought about her struggle with morning sickness, that I know she's briefly mentioned in passing, or her sleepless nights.

Since becoming a mum myself, I see the way the cycle goes. Our babies don't appreciate that we don't sleep for what feels like a lifetime. They don't see the time we spend calming their cries, or how we put every element of our own lives on the back burner forevermore. You can guarantee they feel it, though. They feel it when they hug you and it feels like home. They feel it when they fall and you're the person they reach for. They feel it when something great happens and their eyes dart to you, to check if you saw it, too.

We don't want praise. Our love is unconditional, and praise comes in the form of loving them, and them loving us. Some days, motherhood is one big jumble of making it look as though we have our sh*t together, even when we don't. I'm grateful to my mum for instilling this thought process into me. Today, I'm taking a moment to appreciate the tricky times she's been through, then swept under the carpet to make sure she looks like she has everything together.

Until I Became a Mum

If I'm honest, I didn't appreciate your sacrifice
Or venture to imagine all you went through
As a teenager, I slammed doors in your face
Now I wish I'd stopped
And just said "thank you"

Because I didn't see the way your world changed
Though I bet you were so happy about it
I didn't see your tears behind closed doors
I only saw your highlights reel
I only saw your best bits

I didn't acknowledge all you gave
All you continue to give
Now I see
That of the entire iceberg
I only saw the tip

I didn't see your never-ending days
All I saw was you
My built-in best friend, my protector, my home
Never a tired, emotional human
Not until I became a mum, too

I never saw your sleepless nights
I'll never recall your aching bones
Yet I'll forever feel the love you gave
A hug from you
Still feels like home

Here I am sharing similar experiences
Giving birth is no joke

No doubt your confidence was knocked
As the maternal body
Changes
Shrinks
And grows

I used to wonder why you'd stare at me
You'd look at me and not look away
As my maternal eyes show me your view
I see now that you were taking a moment
To appreciate the miracle you made

You've never told me how much your life changed
You've never asked for praise
"Don't spend your money
On a present for me", you say
"Just a card on my birthday"

Now, alongside the tip of the iceberg
I see the bottom, middle and top
I see that whilst your little ones are little
You're swept around in a whirlwind
That rarely stops

I knew you gave so much
Yet
I had no idea
Of all you went through
Not until I had a baby of my own
Not until
I became a mum, too.

WEEK 44

We found our happy place

We're happy people, united in our love for the best cakes, shakes and comfort food in all the land. Pull up a seat beneath the fairy-light-entwined vines.

When you're on maternity leave, you find those special people and places that will forever hold a nostalgic place in your heart; the spaces and faces that will one day fill your head with memories that make your feelings dance – just like the old-fashioned sweet shop I used to visit with my mum and grandma. It once stood proud as a sugary symbol of happiness and content family time. In my memory, that confectionary store is an emblem of the days before school and routine could bulldoze through the carefree times spent with my family. Years later, seeing the windows boarded and graffiti smearing the walls was a shock. The memories still exist, but it's sad to see a scene that once formed a magical segment of my childhood, now derelict. Gone. A tangible sign of the passing of time.

Maternity leave has led me to find my grown-up version of that old-fashioned sweet shop – except this is a café. It has an atmosphere of its own, which somehow re-captures a magical element of the olden days. The ones you see in black-and-white films, where the world ticked by at a calmer pace, humans seemed kinder, and calories didn't count. We're at Vinnies. No apostrophe needed – the name refers to those who dwell here. I'm a Vinnie, she's a Vinnie, he's a Vinnie, they're a Vinnie. We're happy people, united in our love for the best cakes, shakes and comfort food in all the land. How lucky are we, that this café is humbly nestled in our local town of Northwich? Pull up a seat beneath the fairy-light-entwined vines. Fittingly, I recommend the "Nostalgia" hot chocolate. Laced with butterscotch and toffee sauce, it tastes so illegally delicious.

Maybe that's why even the teenagers seem happier here. When the owner says: "Sorry for your wait, darling", the teenage boy doesn't shrug and shuffle off; he beams her a smile and replies: "It's really no problem", before heading on his jolly way. Then there's the children. They say please and thank you with excitement across their little faces. Probably because this is where we find the best desserts any of us have ever tasted. Over the changing seasons, I've noticed people arriving here under a rainbow of varying moods and circumstances. Some appear looking carefree and sun-kissed; others wrangle with storm-beaten umbrellas in a race to gobble lunch; then there's the ones who have their shoulders hunched towards their ears and look like they need a hug in a mug. They came to the right place. Once they're in, their silhouettes relax as they melt into a chair.

It seems one glance at Vinnies' cake-filled glass cabinet can calm anyone down. It certainly makes me feel calmer and happier. Sometimes in our garden room, the lack of normality feels unsettling. The exciting adventure of shed life clashes with moments of discomfort, just as my baby's nap times clash with the cacophony of power tools screeching in the background as our future home is built. Vinnies is the perfect antidote to that. It's become a consistent comfort blanket when these often up-in-the-air days have felt overwhelming. A treasured escape.

Back to the present moment and our tummies are full. The frustration I arrived with seems to have risen alongside the clouds of steam from my coffee and dispersed into nothing. We've had perhaps a little too much to eat and drink, yet I'm still not ready to leave. I don't want to walk out of the jingly door that leads from this Narnia, into the real world. The people on the other side are less friendly and the food will never be so deliciously naughty.

Plus, my baby is mesmerised by the way this micro-world buzzes by. He enjoys listening to the ice cream machine as it whips up sundae-style milkshakes that fill dessert glasses. They're piled high with cream and treats, then drizzled with sweet sauce. He's infatuated by the celebration cakes that are carried out to a harmony of "ahhh"s and "wow"s from an impressed crowd of customers. His innocent eyes reflect the warm glow of fairylit faux vines that line the ceiling as he gazes at the buttercream-swirled cupcakes beside the counter. During this moment of calm, I welcome an opportunity for reflection. I note how much he's changed. Those dark almond eyes now display a greater sense of alertness and intrigue than they did the first time we visited Vinnies. They're framed with defined eyebrows, softened with curls dancing across his forehead.

Earlier, someone asked how old he is and I realised I've been having the same conversation with different people for around ten months now, yet the only variant each time is his age. "How old is he?" Two weeks, four weeks, four months, eight months. This time, I feel shocked by the way my mouth forms the words "nearly eleven months". How did we get to almost eleven months? Our first irreplaceable year is drawing to a close. I think about my first year of motherhood so far and how much my life has changed – for the better. I've stepped off the corporate hamster wheel, carved out a freelance career, learned all about asserting boundaries, equipped myself with a few motherhood-meddler management skills and of course, discovered the meaning of maternal love – all whilst navigating my ongoing journey with PMDD. Without a doubt, this has been my most pivotal year yet.

I'm back in the room as I hear a lady reading a text out loud to her children. "Daddy says 'Where is this magical café and why am I not there?'" It's a fair point. For the rollercoaster we ride during pregnancy and motherhood, I'm grateful that fellow mums and I get to enjoy this calm slice of paradise. It sweetens the sometimes-bitter edges of our sleepless nights and often knocked-over emotions. We deserve it.

Of course, it's not just mums here. Another ingredient in the magic of Vinnies is the eclectic mix of people. This café breaks through the boundaries of generational and social divides, bringing everyone together through a love of happy vibes, comforting food, decent music and tasty treats. There's the friendly guy with the pink mohawk, the old man reading his newspaper and the lady who looks like she's just popped out for five minutes of peace. There's the husband-and-husband duo who I often see coming in for a sandwich with their dog, the gentleman whose order we know off-by-heart: "A Guardians of the Galaxy milkshake please, and I'll wait outside because my son's out there". Plus, the lady who's often here on the same days as me, which is very regularly. We exchange a warm, knowing smile each time – from one Vinnies addict to another. Our hearts and tummies are full of happiness and we return to our garden room feeling refreshed. These are the days we'll remember.

Vinnies

There's this special place we've found
It's like Narnia came to Northwich

Food wraps you in comfort
You'll find joy nestled in a sandwich

Behind the door, people are kinder
Children's manners are flawless
Happy folks gather to chat, read, relax
Underscored by a foot-tapping playlist

It's not just a café
It's our home when life feels frantic
Where ingredients go into a milkshake jug
And problems are solved like magic

This place blurs the generational divide
The old and young are one
We've made friends with lovely ladies and gents
They play peekaboo with my son

When motherhood knocks me over
This is where I'll find my balance and sit
If there's one humble, homely, heaven on earth
I'm pretty sure we've found it

By the counter is the place to be
The scenes will have you mesmerised
Handmade cakes ready to be delivered
Treats you can taste with your eyes

Everyone watches the animation
As comfort food is served and milkshakes are made
Dainty triangular sandwiches
Dance across the little ones' plates

I want to capture these days in a snow globe
Revisit them forever
Because when we're all old and our babies are grown
These moments will become nostalgia

Once strangers, now friends
This community has watched my baby grow
I feel this magical place
Helps everyone more
Than its owners will ever know.

WEEK 45

The importance of identity

It seems commonplace to be fighting the idea that we exist as everything to everyone and nobody to ourselves.

It sounded all-at-once funny, foreign, and magical being called "Mum" for the first time at hospital check-ups. And so, it began. It started as a beautiful word that captured my upcoming status and tied it in a bow. Next, it naturally morphed into a label that seemingly cancelled my needs and placed them onto my newborn. This is the iteration of the word that I'm content with; I love having my little one at the centre of everything I do. I'll happily fit myself around the edges, wherever there's room. Finally, though, just as I was getting to grips with motherhood, the mum label grew legs and that's when I've found myself at the centre of other peoples' expectations. If I go along with those expectations, my identity slips away in the process and there's no room left for me. Not even to squidge myself in around the edges. If I set boundaries to push back on those expectations, I'm the bad guy. Not Jamie, not those who try to break our sanity-saving boundaries – me.

It seems commonplace to be fighting the idea that we exist as everything to everyone and nobody to ourselves. I've spoken about this with many fellow parents. When I first became a mum, I made it my mission to extend my nurturing arms to those who appeared to feel left behind – or who I had been told directly, felt pushed out. I wanted everyone to feel involved, special, and to have equal time with our little love. I also felt embarrassed that the matriarchal baton had been passed to me and that I was consuming a large amount of attention that I hadn't asked for.

My home became the hive of activity as people helpfully rallied around us. Most family and friends were respectfully looking to me as the deciding factor when it came to certain arrangements. I'd inadvertently taken on a special new role as chief decision-maker and couldn't fathom why. Through the experience of motherhood, I've realised that I'm supported to make decisions based on what's best for our family, because new families tend to have a routine and fresh traditions to make. Most were happy with us setting our own routines and traditions – others weren't. For those who weren't happy, I burned myself out in the process of breaking my own boundaries, driving a digger through my baby's routine and putting the onus on me to ensure they felt fulfilled and got to enjoy equal time with him if they didn't want to work around us. This turned out to be a mistake. A mistake that felt suffocating.

The more I continued to mould myself to fit into the schedules of others, the more I was expected to mould. The more energy I gave, the more was taken. The more time I mustered up out of nowhere, the more time I was expected to continue mustering up out of nowhere. In the process, there was simply no space left for me. I can't change where people live or whether they're open to visiting beyond their own schedules or not. I can't force people to visit during the times that suit our boundaries when they complain of not seeing him enough. Likewise, I refuse to continue pushing my own needs even further down the list to prioritise the preferences of others. It was impacting my health. My PMDD went on a downwards spiral as I suffered with the mental exhaustion of trying to spin all the plates at once. Why should I push myself aside to suit people beyond our immediate family, simply because I became a parent?

I had two choices: ditch my own needs and quit my career to take on the full-time role of making sure everyone who wanted to see my baby on their own schedule, could see him whenever they wanted to, without fitting around our boundaries. This would mean I'd "keep the peace" for everyone else but lose myself, precious bonding time with my son, and my career in the process. Not a good idea. Alternatively, option two – the sensible option – meant setting a structure that struck a smart balance of bonding time with my baby and prioritising myself during his nap times. I chose the latter, peaceful route. I chose it without explanation or apology and I turned my back on the backlash.

Instead, I focused on making positive changes. Upon realising that a huge part of my identity was my writing career, that became my starting point on my mission to reclaim my sense of self. Thanks to my achievements to-date, my healthy portfolio of samples, experience and keen clients have all made it possible to continue writing in a freelance capacity, that allows me to work on my terms, around my family. So, instead of returning to full-time employment after maternity leave, I recently launched my writing career on a freelance basis – and finally found a balance that works. Without asserting my boundaries and making space for my own identity, this goal never would have been achieved.

For every decision I make for my family, it seems there'll be someone there to tell me that it doesn't work for them. It often feels like for every opportunity I choose to pursue, there's someone dropping their poo-filled bag of problems on my doorstep and telling me to pick it up, sort it out and polish it off. There was a time when I'd have happily taken that bag without gloves and arranged everything to perfection before handing the solved puzzle back smelling of baby powder. Nowadays, I'll peacefully launch that bag back in the direction it came from, put my blinkers on, zone out of the background noise and continue doing what's best for myself and my family. Happy mum, happy baby. I take on just the right amount of work to ensure I achieve a harmonious blend of mum life, work life and me-time – and I know I'm lucky to do so. In turn, for the first time in a while, I recognise a small segment of myself again and am excited for my future, both as a mum and as a woman with an identity beyond motherhood.

New mums are entitled to nurture their own identity in whichever form they choose. They're entitled to alone time, to sleep, to embrace their own hobbies in the time they have left over – which usually is very little, if any. It was a culture shock to discover that having a baby meant I needed to fight for these simple things that once came peacefully to me. Every new mum, no matter the circumstances or who manipulates them into thinking otherwise, is entitled to her own daily or weekly structure and to say "no" to others, unapologetically and without explanation.

Of course, not all women have to fight for their identity. Not everybody has to wriggle from the grip of outside demands. Maybe there are women who face no pressure at all. Perhaps others like it. For those subjected to it without wanting to be, I believe it's dangerous. In the process of writing this book, I've spoken to women whose children grew up a long time ago, and they've found themselves suffering a complete loss of identity with no idea on where to even look for it.

What I find so damaging about women being stripped of their identities throughout motherhood is the impact it has on them once their children have grown. If you pin your entire sense of purpose and identity onto the shoulders of one tiny human, what happens when that human grows? Perhaps you could have another one but inevitably, that human will grow, too. I feel every mum should be given the time, space and grace to figure out what makes her, her – whether that's a career, a hobby, a housewife role, or a daily bubble bath. For me, it was the space to re-build myself and my career.

Once again, motherhood has replaced my mouse squeak with a lion's roar. For the first time ever, I'm standing up for myself and my family, asserting boundaries, finding my identity and in the process, beginning to thrive in motherhood. This journey isn't easy and I feel modern society isn't wired to support new mothers but I'll continue to fight against the pressures that tell me to be everything to everyone and nobody to myself. I hope that my son subconsciously takes note of this journey and that his gender will never be limited to certain hobbies or tasks.

I'll raise him with the knowledge that both sexes have equal opportunities and equal rights to an identity of their own – whether or not children are involved. I hope that he'll grow up with the knowledge that both sexes are entitled to the joys of earning money, enjoying hobbies, and maintaining or even growing their identities – if they want to. I'll continue to fight against unhealthy demands on my time. I won't spend nap times driving around instead of resting or working towards my dreams, so someone can have my baby delivered to them. Motherhood isn't about pleasing others. Since choosing this peaceful route, I'm thriving in modern motherhood.

Modern Motherhood

"Not cooking every night for the family?
This woman is no good"

Actually, your checklist is outdated
I'm thriving in modern motherhood

I don't hide in the shadows
I'm a human, too

The amount I love my family
Doesn't make my needs less valued

My son won't grow up thinking
That women live in the shadows

I'll show him that a mum, too, can have superpowers
Victory is a feeling that Dad *and* Mum knows

I'm his dad's number one cheerleader
And I get the same back from him

My boy will know that regardless of gender
Anyone can do anything

I don't exist to appease others
I wasn't born to iron shirts

I'm juggling my career, my hobbies, my family
I've found a balance that works

So leave your comments in your head
I don't need outdated advice

And yes, I'll continue to assert my independence
After I've become a wife

Because parenthood enhances me
But never will it define me

I'm a career woman, a dream-catcher, a fiery spirit
And yes – *also* the proud mum to my family

My needs will not lay dormant
My dreams will not be pushed aside

My voice will not go unheard
I hope my child one day views that with pride

Because we do it the modern way

His dad and me

We're all about raising a family
Grown with love, teamwork, equality

Whether or not Eve
Was made from Adam's rib

I'm a human with rights and feelings
My needs are as important as his

My time is not a plaything
My love cannot be bought

My ambitions will be achieved
With or without support

And when I need space for my needs to be met
The answer isn't a "no" or "maybe"

We interchange our roles with equality
And these are the values we will maintain
In our modern family.

WEEK 46

A sea of support

Those helping hands through testing times took my friendships and relationships to a deeper level than before.

Since I had my baby – even since I got pregnant – I've grown closer with people I didn't think I could grow any closer to. Through the throes of morning sickness, recovering from birth and sleepless nights, I saw a sea of support in the form of understanding hands. There were people who made it their mission to help, or even to carry out random acts of kindness. Like the friend who brought chocolates for me alongside the baby gifts. "Mum needs looking after, too", she said. I didn't expect gestures like this but at a time when I felt vulnerable, I'll forever remember them.

Whilst some of my relationships grew stronger, others took a battering. Some people wanted my baby, but not me. Others wanted me, but not my baby. Some cared for us both – and these are the friendships that are flourishing. On my journey to stop pressing the self-destruct button on friendships, I've learned that it is also okay to step back from the ones that no longer serve you both. It's nothing personal. Life isn't one linear line; it's a journey of twists and turns, ups and downs, backwards and forwards, with a few lost and found friends and funky chicken dances along the way. You can't beat those friendships that are fortified throughout parenthood, though. There's something about the sight of an understanding hand when you need it the most, that you treasure in your heart forever.

Those helping hands through testing times took my friendships and relationships to a deeper level than before. Of course, my relationship with Jamie was already strong. It grew stronger throughout pregnancy and birth, taking on a form of companionship that I didn't know was possible. He held my hand through labour. He took my hand in the middle of the night when I was touching the bottom depths of exhaustion, crying next to my baby's cot in harmony with his half-hourly cries. He took my hand each morning as he lifted my weary body out of bed when I couldn't feel my tummy muscles. Then there were the NHS carers who dramatically enhanced all three of our lives with their care. These understanding hands inevitably disappeared as quickly as they reached out but I'll remember them forever. Though our midwives, nurses and health visitors will probably never remember me, they've been through my biggest, most vulnerable life moments by my side and will forever hold a special place in my memory.

What struck me the most about the care we received from our midwife, Martyne, is the way her understanding hands branched far beyond the role she was paid to carry out. I expected her to do things like monitor our baby's heartbeat and administer the right medication to me, but I never ventured to imagine her staying long beyond her shift had ended to continue her support into the grand finale – to meet our baby in theatre. When we moved from the midwifery-led unit to the consultant-led suite during the 43rd hour of labour, Martyne helped Jamie to set the room up with faux candles, fairy lights and my soothing playlist as though it were her own home. On Jamie's 50th waking hour, she made a beanbag bed where he could catch fifty winks to help him power through the rest of our birth. Her support was unwavering.

Whether it was from my fiancé, my midwife, health visitor, closest friends, sister, or my dad, I felt as though I was being lifted up by all the understanding hands that clubbed together to help throughout early parenthood. Their support extended beyond anything I could have imagined.

An Understanding Hand

I enjoy the creativity of life through my eyes
Though it can sometimes seem a challenge
Whilst others see the world through world-tinted lenses
Mine have added colour
They're sparkling
Effervescent

Sometimes the colour drains and those sparkling scenes turn dark
And murky
And dull
Then an understanding hand appears
Offering a safe platform
In place of a fall

Trish the health visitor
She came to see me and my newborn baby
As she held my hand in hers
I realised I'll never forget the kindness
The helping hands
Of this lady

Memories of holding my mum's hand
I plodded happily next to her, most of the time
As soon as a car
A roaming dog
A stranger appeared
Her hand would grab mine

An unspoken symbol of safety
A sign that someone cares
A simple gesture to say it all
When the words
Aren't always there

Now here's my fiancé
The only man who's ever
Tried
To understand
The more force I used to push him away
The further he reached out his hand

In the early days, I expected him to leave
I wanted to be alone
Yet he urged me to see there's stability to be found
In having that one person
Who won't let you tackle tricky things on your own

He listed the parts of my mind he could relate to
Overwhelmed, foggy, pushing friends away
Then taking my hand in his, he said
"I'm different and I want to help you

I'll prove it
If you let me stay"

Years of not knowing what these feelings were
GPs with vacant expressions
Yet in the hospital
Striving to soothe my mind like it was their own
My baby's dad and our midwives
Turned our hospital room into my home

If it wasn't for becoming a mum
I'm not sure I'd have found a professional who understands
The mental health midwife explained each detail of our birthing space
She set the scene as though I could feel it
With my very own hands

After the birth, our health visitor
Points out the sense of order
And purity in my home
Then clasps my hand in hers and says
"Did you know you've found a talent
Through your need to feel calm
And in control?"

It's because my home softens the tricky times
Like when I'm breaking out of these moulds made by others
Pushing back against outdated stereotypes
Bending the bars that are put on women
Simply because they became mothers

My stepdad notices the pressure I've been under
Since I had my son
Emotionally drained and tired all the time
He takes my hand in his and says
"Never forget you're an amazing mum"

Wish I still had the safety of my grandma's hands

Magic blue veins and wrinkles
Their healing properties were incredible
Through the good, bad, sad and scary times
Her hands were where mine would nestle

Now my baby is toddling
He walks like E.T
And he's plodding happily next to me most of the time
Just as I think my heart couldn't feel fuller
I feel a tiny hand grab mine.

WEEK 47

Making the most of every moment

I'll embrace every single sunrise and sunset, because one day, the house will fall silent, his dad and I will wake up refreshed, and we won't have our baby waking next to us. He'll be grown.

Stroking my baby to sleep, I reflect on the day: everything he's found funny, the things he's been amazed at, how much he enjoyed his food at tea time. I note the way he smeared it across his face and tummy to get a feel for the textures. What a privilege, to stroke this little love to sleep. He keeps opening his eyes and I could fall asleep myself, as I watch them get heavier, and heavier and … yaaaawn. I've had one of the most wholesome days I can remember – we both have. Yet it still feels like an achievement, to have reached this time of evening unscathed, because there have been a whole bunch of tricky times rolled in with that wholesomeness. It's not the kind of achievement I've ever felt before. This is a feeling of having completed something really quite challenging, but it seems like there's never been anything more worth it, to know that I've poured so much love and care into this new life. I've nourished him with my own milk, entertained him and taught him new things, whilst physically and emotionally exhausted. Hooray for my worn-out body and mind.

On the other hand, this sense of victory is tinged with an awareness that it's another day less of being a mum to a baby. It's another day less of feeling his tiny hands clutch onto mine or having him curled up to my chest in the early hours – eyes closed, his hungry mouth open like a baby bird that's feeling its way around for food. I will miss these days. It's also another day closer to the countless adventures we'll have together when he gets older.

When he learns to walk, we'll crunch through autumn's leaves in our wellies. When he appreciates cosy film nights, we can snuggle in a blanket together in the winter, our hot chocolates piled high with cream and sprinkles. It fills me with gratitude to think of the days that are still ahead of us: when we can chat to him about how his day went and the interests he develops, as his personality continues to grow alongside his never-ending legs. Yes, I'll miss him as a baby, but there's so much left to look forward to.

Back in the moment, his dark eyes keep opening as he fights sleep. I catch them, momentarily glittering in the ray of light that's peeking through the door; underscored by the light thump of music from the garden, as his dad and workmen build our home. We're in a different world to them. They're powered up on coffee and music, whilst we've been winding down with a bubble bath and meditation music. Time seems to have paused for a while, in this bubble of relaxation we seem to have created.

This moment feels profound. I never used to see the beauty in the closing of a day. In my old world of spreadsheets and peer reviews, I didn't care to reflect on anything. Curling up with a book and a family-sized bag of Milky Buttons was all I wanted to do at the end of a long working day. Nowadays, I appreciate every single thing that happened in each set of 24 hours that pass me by – even though I spend most of those 24 hours wide awake, running on adrenaline. Because, though this is our new normal, I will never let this be normal. This is magic, before my eyes. Now, we have sleep. He's recharging, ready for more contradictory profound normality in the morning. I'll embrace every single sunrise and sunset, because one day, the house will fall silent, his dad and I will wake up refreshed, and we won't have our baby waking next to us. He'll be grown.

When the House Falls Silent

When the house falls silent
No cries
No contagious laughter
I bet we'll squirm in those moments of peace
Though peace is often what we're lusting after

When I'm not cleaning concreted cereal off the floor
Not wrestling him to brush his teeth
When I'm not kissing trapped fingers and grazed knees
I'll be aching for the days
Of *him, him, him* – and me

I bet the echoes of his childhood will always ring through our home

We'll be hearing cartoon piggy oinks forever
We'll no longer see mess, dirty nappies, or soiled clothes
We'll remember them fondly
As his precious baby-hood treasure

I'm proud of us, as his mum and dad
Because sometimes when things get tough
We understand that one day we'll miss this
So we march on, fuelled by teamwork
And coffee
And comedy
And love

When the storm tries to knock us over
We forever say "we've got this"
The wind gathers pace and tries to prize us apart
It tugs at my hair and it pulls at your shirt
But
We hold hands through it

We know that one day we'll recline
Into our peaceful, tidy home
And though we'll have each other back
I bet a part of me
And a part of you
Will feel alone

Because when the house falls silent
He won't have kept me awake
Snuffling at my chest
You won't be flying him around the kitchen
Or feel him tugging at your legs

We'll need to set alarms again
We'll miss being the best fun and love he's ever known
We'll dream of holding his tiny hands
We'll wake up searching for them

But those tiny hands
Will be grown

Yes, what a full-on time we're in
It's crazy how hard this sometimes is
But as we've said 100 times over
We've got all we need
There's no one else either of us could do this with

So, we embrace these days
The season of hard work
No sleep
Rainstorms and clouds but mostly sun
The season of identifying
As "Knackered Dad" and "Exhausted Mum"

Because when pocket-sized clothes don't carpet the floor
And his little raincoat doesn't hang on the hook
When we're not tripping over cars and building blocks
It'll be a symbol of times gone by
A sign
That he's
All
Grown
Up.

WEEK 48

Motherhood confessions

When my mum took our newborn photos, I rushed upstairs to curl my hair and put make-up and a nice blouse on. The photographs needed to say: "I'm a new mum and look how well I have everything together".

I don't subscribe to the institution of motherhood. I don't understand what a centile is and I've never been to get my baby weighed outside of a health visitor appointment – nor do I worry about his weight. I rarely feel the "mum guilt" that so many people warned me of (amidst the birth warnings and other pre-defined expectations that others tried to throw at me before my baby had even arrived). I'm unlikely to be rushing around in a grey cloud of stress that people can feel before they see me. I don't want my baby – or my friends and family – to pick up on that. This is the hardest job I've ever had but I'm the happiest I've ever been. Right now, I'm taking each day as it comes and embracing the motherhood journey through sleepy eyes, mum-guilt-free because I know I'm doing my best. The only thing I occasionally feel guilty for is not spreading myself into the pre-built worry mould that society has evidently set up for any mum worth her status. The panicky, stressed, manic mum. Are you even a mum if you aren't rushing around?

It's never just another manic mum-day over here. It's my black-and-white life, now with added colour. It's my calm life, sometimes sped up to a faster pace since my sweet best friend has joined me. It's my straightforward life, often slowed down, to accommodate play time, morning naps, enjoying a lychee for the first time, or enjoying the fresh taste of the strawberries we picked at the farm. Meanwhile, we let society run away with the idea that you're not a mum if you're not a permanently panicking nervous wreck on autopilot. Let's hang back and enjoy the view from over here for a while.

I've never had a sleep-inducing sheep in my baby-bedtime toolbox and I rarely rock or walk my baby to sleep; I breastfeed him, because I'm too lazy to walk around. I'm making a rod for my own back, they say, but I treasure that rod and I'll carry it with pride. Sometimes, I leave him in his cot to cry for a short while, whilst I do one normal thing, like feel a hot shower on my back or the strong rays of our globally warmed sun on my face, though I know it isn't recommended. It's balance.

I've never taken on the housewife role. Jamie mostly cooks tea for both of us whilst I mostly sustain this little life we've created. I rarely iron. I mostly buy baby clothes that don't crease. Life is too short to iron a sleepsuit that's going to get sick on it, in my opinion. I will not let society tell me that's the role I carved out for myself, by becoming a mum. Are you even a mum if you're not fraught with worry and guilt? Yes, you are. You're a calm, happy mum who has the time to cherish the special moments of motherhood. This is a new life that you built from your very own body. This is a little person with a growing personality. Your default best friend, who will share the highs and the lows of life with you, taking the highs even higher and adding a dash of sweetness to the bitter taste of bad times.

I didn't get married before having a baby. I'm not religious and I won't get him christened. He was planned for the future, but then came as a surprise. The best surprise we've ever had. We dreamt about him so much that we manifested him a little earlier than expected and now we can see why he was so meant to be. My baby has never had a nursery. We moved house when he was four months old and the majority of his first year has been spent in a garden room that his dad built in one week.

I've never had a breastfeeding chair to rock him to sleep in, or a side table with personalised baby paraphernalia on, like the ones you see on Instagram. He's never had a cushion with his name and birth date embroidered on it. I rarely buy him special, personalised things because I'm an overly emotional, sentimental minimalist and I know once that object comes into my life, I'll keep hold of it forever and I don't want to have a loft full of special things that I never look at but can't get rid of.

I never had a professional pregnancy photoshoot or a newborn family photoshoot. When my mum took our newborn photos, I rushed upstairs to curl my hair and put make-up and a nice blouse on. The photographs needed to say: "I'm a new mum and look how well I have everything together". The moment the camera was put down, so too was my fake image. I washed my face and was back in my scar-friendly pyjamas within minutes.

My life has been turned upside down but it turns out that upside down was the right way around all along. The sleepless nights are here to test me, but I'm in control of the pace, the way I react to challenges and my ability to make every day a calm, happy mum-day. I can rush this season in a grey cloud of stress as is often the expectation for parents, or I can be mindful and ground myself in this series of mundane and magical moments, soaking in every second. I choose the latter. Because these are the days I'll look back on with nostalgia. These are the days I'd like to preserve between the pages of a fairytale and treasure forever.

These Are the Days

These are the days
I'll look back on with nostalgia
I'm full of emotion, I'm overprotective
Couldn't be any prouder

Long walks
Strangers stopping to admire him
Old people pinging his curls
Complimenting me on the outfit he's dressed in

Our walks led to making new friends all summer
I'll never forget to appreciate it
I love to watch the non-working generations blend together
Old ladies are my favourite

The smell of fresh pastry as we pass the bakery
Watching the sun glint on the canal as we cross the lock
The sense of calm in the library
Sharing a toastie with my boy in "our" coffee shop

We sit amongst other parents in cafés
As well as old people and remote workers
We frequent these places so often
People recognise and speak to us

Our walks have become our daily ritual
A way to mark his growth

He’s sat up, laughing with me now
His newborn body slept in a carrycot a few months ago

These are my final weeks of “this time last year I was pregnant”
When I couldn’t imagine what it would be like to be a mum
I spent month nine in my home-made grotto watching Christmas films
Unaware of the joy
And love
And craziness to come

I never imagined I’d be blessed with him
The salamander smiling up from his pram
Laughing at the pelican crossing
When the red turns into a green man

I didn’t realise our relationship would have such depth
My picnic-in-the-park companion from March to September
Crunching through autumn’s auburn leaves
Feeling winter’s chill on our noses in November

We’ve discovered new places
I’d never have enjoyed on my own
Like Baby Bounce, Rhyme Time and the sensory café
All an adventure-packed walk from our home

He's my faithful companion who’s been by my side
For every second of the crazy adventure in our garden room
He's grown from a tiny baby to a one-year-old here
We'll be moving into our home soon

But these are the days I’ll remember
The sink baths
The never-ending nappies
His contagious baby laugh

One day when he’s grown
Only memories and nostalgia will remain

I'll wish I had him reaching up to me
To feel these chubby thighs in his sleepsuit again

And this is why I live these days to the fullest
No time to be sidetracked
Because one day I'll reach for his tiny hand
And that tiny hand
Won't reach back.

WEEK 49

When our roads branch in different directions

I understand that one day, he'll embark upon his own journey. We'll reach a natural fork in our road, where his branches one way and mine will be forced to take a different route.

My son will always be my baby, even when he's a grown man. Yet, I understand that his needs will grow and change with him. One day he won't need feeding, holding up on the slide, or snuggles in a blanket before bed, but I hope the instinct I have for nurturing him as a baby will flow through to his adulthood. I hope the "right" thing to do just comes to me in whatever situation we find ourselves in, as it does now. But I'm sure the future will hold some tricky times amidst the happy ones – his first argument with a friend, his first heartbreak, or the first time his confidence is knocked.

One day, there's a high chance he'll fall in love and I won't be the one his eyes search for in a crowded room anymore. I hope I can graciously step back, find yet another version of my own identity, and leave him to his own life in the knowledge that I'll always be there for him if and when he needs me. Both Jamie and I will. I hope that he and/or his potential future family don't ever feel pressure from me to fill the him-shaped gap in my life. Because all I want is the best for him.

Life is a series of profound and mundane moments strung together. I find that every three months or so, I'm adapting to a new or slightly different era of my life, whether that's a new job, a new baby class, a new phase that my little one's in, or a new challenge I've taken on. Some changes are big, others are miniscule, but there's no doubt that things are constantly changing. I can't imagine the day when the big change comes: the one where my boy doesn't need me anymore.

I know it's inevitable. I understand that one day, he'll embark upon his own journey. We'll reach a natural fork in our road, where his branches one way and mine will be forced to take a different route. I'll need to make an effort to add some exciting landmarks along my new route. To find new focuses in my life and new hobbies to make sure I'm not still pinning all my time and social life on him. His dad and I will focus on us again. There won't be a tiny coat on the hook, an intricately woven map of toys to tell the tale of his little imagination, or Playdough stuck to our furniture. It'll be sad and I'll miss it. Even so, I'll commit to taking a step back. I'll leave him to live his own life, in the hope that our invisible umbilical cord will continue to ping back again whenever he needs me. All I want is for him to be happy, on whichever path he chooses. All I want is the best for him.

The Best for You

Never before has it been normal
To wake with feet pattering across my face
To have someone's hands in my mouth
Or their salty tears to taste

Never before has it been normal
To stare at somebody this way
To trace every curve and dimple
And with eye contact; not look away

Never before has it been normal
To wipe somebody else's nose
To remove sleep from the creases of their eyes
Or fluff from between their toes

Never before has it been normal
To watch somebody sleep
These moments would all seem strange
If you weren't an extension of me

Never again do I want to be without
This love I get up every single day for
The tugging at my leg
The food that punctuates the floor

Because though I may sigh internally

This is treasure, not mess
One day it'll be nostalgia
In a rogue building block
I'll see happiness

I'll miss tracing that map of toys
The treasure hunt that has you at the end
One day I'll reach the end of the road
And there won't sit my little friend

But one day when you're grown
I'll find yet another new version of myself
I'm sure I'll miss you until it hurts
But that won't be a worry for you or anybody else

This is something I need to write down
To immortalise on paper
Whichever path you choose for your life
I promise
I won't be a meddler

I won't be trying to heal my wounds
I won't be fighting to fill my empty nest
I won't be scrambling to hog the spotlight
Hoping that your new family will love me the best

I'll take an elegant step back
Because this will be your time
Your time to spend with your family
Just as I did, with mine

Because never before has it been normal
To love someone this way
All I want is the best for you
Every single day.

WEEK 50

The chapter of exponential growth

Motherhood has been the best, most wholesome experience I could ever venture to imagine. The tricky bit has been how the entire world as I knew it changed.

As I begin to wrap up my last week of living in a shed, my baby's final days as a 0-year-old and my early Christmas shopping, I'm also beginning to wrap up my first year of motherhood. We've almost come full circle. This has been one looping rollercoaster of a year and it's given me more confidence and strength of character than I ever could have imagined. I'd like to capture everything I've learned from research, learned from someone else, learned through a happy accident, or fell flat on my face and learned through sheer need, during my first year of life as a mum like this.

In the early days, I didn't think I was coping with the outside demands that tumbled down upon me once I became a mum. In hindsight, I'd been dealing with them really well. The pressures that got thrown my way were a lot for any modern mum to deal with and it turns out, I wasn't alone. I've since met a whole network of women who are enjoying being mums, whilst grappling with the outside demands of motherhood itself. I'm not the only one who has struggled with being under the motherhood microscope. I've learned that often, it's not becoming a mum that many of us find hard. Motherhood has been the best, most wholesome experience I could ever venture to imagine. The tricky bit has been how the entire world as I knew it changed. From the moment I shared the result of that positive pregnancy test, the landscape of my life shifted. At some points, my time became a free-for-all.

Everything from my home to my body became a topic up for discussion. People's attitudes towards me changed. My role as a woman changed. Inevitably, the way I now view and deal with the world around me has changed. It had to. This felt like a sink or swim situation. With the help of a few armbands and floats from my friends and family, I've transformed from a floundering fish out of water, to a mermaid who can now elegantly swim through the sometimes turbulent yet forever rewarding ocean of motherhood – with PMDD. Finding my way through the world as a mum like this has empowered me to grow stronger. For the first time in my adult life, I set boundaries, stand up for myself, and step back from unhealthy environments and expectations. I'd never have been forced to do this, had I not become a parent.

From my PMDD diagnosis to the pressures that seemed to fall on me from every angle, I'm thankful for each transformative stop-off on my journey to becoming a mum like this. I see now that all along, the world has been preparing me for this chapter: the chapter of exponential growth. Everything that came before, has been building me up for this period of my life; where everything from my body to my mindset and the way I spend my time, has changed. If I could have my time as a new mum again, or even if we ever have another baby in the future, I'd like to remember the lessons I've learned the first time around – and all the things I would tell my pre-baby self.

20 lessons I've learned as a mum like this

1. You can maintain a clean home whilst comfortably raising a baby, if that's something that's important to you. Whilst those in week one warned of the perils of a cream sofa, this year has proven that all I needed was a few decent cleaning products.
2. Always follow your instinct. If you ever feel unsure about something or simply don't want to do it, you're allowed to say "no".
3. During pregnancy and early motherhood in particular, remember to put your blinkers on when needed. People will want to fill your mind with their ideas of pregnancy and motherhood. Remember that your instinct tends to be the best advice.
4. If you're able to, sink into and soak up those early days of motherhood. It's like a second chance at becoming a teenager and throwing adult routines out of the window. Grasp it with both hands.
5. Remember to pay forward the kindness that people gave to you during pregnancy and motherhood. At what can be a confusing time, extending an understanding hand can enhance someone

else's experience of motherhood. That's the kind of kindness they'll remember forever.

6. Lows will forever be interwoven with highs – work with every feeling you have and you'll flourish.
7. On any days that look grim, remind yourself of your safe home and everything else you have to be grateful for. Never lose sight of how lucky you are for raising your child against a backdrop of peace.
8. Motherhood is one long list of contradictions. Where possible, let yourself be carried away and swirled around in whichever direction your life wants to take you, without resistance.
9. Having a baby often highlights the absence of those we love the most.
10. It's okay to blend the best parts of traditional and modern parenting to suit you.
11. You're not here to mother anyone except your baby. Nobody else's happiness should ever depend on you and if someone isn't happy, you don't need to fix it. That was a myth you learned in childhood. You can let go of that now.
12. Boundaries. People might try to push them but it's up to you to re-assert them. Once you've asserted them, don't be afraid to step back. Your sanity is more important than others' demands or expectations.
13. Finding comfort in sadness is powerful. We're not raised to be okay with feeling unhappy. Embrace the lows as much as the highs.
14. It's okay to enjoy being alone. This is your life and no one else has the right to lay claim to it.
15. Social media. Once you've popped, society will make it hard for you to stop. Use the apps to your advantage but don't let them use you.
16. Don't make excuses. There's nothing wrong with saying "we need family time" or "I'm not feeling up to it". Happy parents, happy baby.
17. Those who want to spend time with your baby will fit into his life – not the other way around. Make sure visitors know they're welcome at the times that suit you and leave it at that.

18. When you know it's time to leave, leave. Nobody else feeds and rocks your baby in the middle of the night. Do what's best for you and your family.
19. Motherhood is the hardest, yet most rewarding and wholesome job you've ever done. Now you can do anything.
20. Don't worry about losing your identity throughout motherhood. Most people do. You'll find your feet again.

Perhaps the most valuable of all lessons that I learned this year, was that feeling overwhelmed whilst trying to mother your baby and rediscover your identity in a culture that often celebrates new mums and then watches them struggle – is *normal.* It shouldn't be normal, but for that struggle, I'm thankful, in many ways. My world has grown a bolder, brighter, stronger place because of it. Now, let's get ready to finally flee the garden room in favour of a home and close off this first year of motherhood.

One

This is one heck of a journey
This is one long, wild ride
Willing the tricky times to speed past
Wishing to freeze this entire period of time

It's been one year of contradictions
Often wondering when we'll next sleep
Nine pregnant months followed by one year of love
That feels so wholesome
That runs so deep

As we roll into this final month
Motherhood seems even more profound
Memories of this year flick through my mind
Like an old-fashioned film reel with no sound

This has been one life-changing year
Filled with things I've never done before
Supporting a tiny fragile body

Now, helping that body to walk

I’ve watched this salamander unravel
Like a flat-packed teddy that took a while to inflate
He was curled into the position of my womb for a while
Now his legs and back are straight

I'm one emotional human
With one heart bursting with love
Wish his great-grandma was here for this chapter
I hope she's watching from above

What a pleasure to see him grow
My tiny 6lb son
He’s transformed from a kidney bean
This month, he’s turning one

One year of guiding him into life
Sometimes to others’ dismay
Holding him "too" near
But I intend to stay close forever
Until the day he guides me out of here.

WEEK 51

Final days of living in the garden

This is the year we became a team, threw caution to the wind and jumped headfirst into a world of unknowns.

This adventure has been fun, but there's only so long you can live in a shed with a baby. As I walk around our soon-to-be new home, I see the kitchen being installed, the fireplace standing proud in the front room, and light fittings being wired in. It doesn't feel real that we'll soon be living a life beyond the flamingo walks to get into bed (if you were with me through week twenty-six, you'll know). These final days of house-building scenes are spotlighting how far we've come since those comfy, cosy days of nesting during the build-up to birth. I was nervous to pack up my calm, Carrie Bradshaw-inspired sanctuary that I called home and exchange it for the unknowns of becoming a mum. I feel worlds away from those days of my baby kicking and twirling in my tummy as I enjoyed milky buttons, hot chocolates, milkshakes, milk and more milk, whilst the house filled with the comforting tones of Alan Titchmarsh. It feels like the earth was moved from beneath my feet for a while, but I've grown stronger this year, without a doubt.

Amidst the huge changes in my life, many things will stay the same as they once were. Just like in week one, our surroundings will still be cosy and soft to comfort my mind, but the scandi interiors were left at Jack Lane. In this period property, I've found an extra element of comfort in dark wood furniture. I've become a nerd for all things mortise and dovetail joints and appreciate the comfort that comes from old, quality, antique furniture that looks like it belonged in my grandma's or great-grandma's house. In fact, some of our furniture did come from their homes, filling mine with a sense of comfort and familiarity. Interior therapy at its finest.

This is the house that, just like motherhood, stands proud as a symbol of another huge achievement that's filled with contradictions. This is the year of house building and first-time parenting. Without a doubt, it's been our hardest, happiest, toughest year yet. This is the year of our biggest adventure. For me, it's the year of being thrown into grown-up-hood, largely on my own – holding a few very special understanding hands for support along the way. It's the year I gained a diagnosis for the PMDD I'd be struggling with for 21 years. For Jamie, it's the year of knocking down walls, re-building, extending and supporting his family. This is the year we became a team, threw caution to the wind and jumped headfirst into a world of unknowns. This is the adventure-packed, rollercoaster life we chose. This is teamwork. This is the house that Dad built.

The House That Dad Built

A couple of years ago
I dreamt of a beautiful home
Not sure exactly who resided there
But it seemed so unlike mine
Where I lived on my own

It had a livelier presence
It looked like a family dwelled there
Toys on the floor
Memories captured in frames
A gallery wall inviting you upstairs

I was intrigued by a picture on the wall
Hanging by a chain, with a slight tilt
I took a closer look
It's a drawing of this family home
And it's titled:
"The House That Dad Built"

I looked around some more
A fireplace stands tall in greyish black
Brass and glass chandelier in the hallway
Shades of white on the walls
A country kitchen at the back

I was fascinated by this cosy nest
A place I'd like to stay for biscuits and tea
To snuggle on the sofa in a blanket

Breakfast at the island
Watch the rain patter down from the window seat

Through feathered edges
I glimpsed someone who lived here
But I could only see his back
So I floated to the front of him
And my future husband stood there smiling
You're this home's happy dad?

Now, a couple of years later, I'm awake
That dream has come to life
My baby's dad is finishing that very home
It's the house that Dad built
For his son and soon-to-be wife

Within these bricks and mortar
Memories will be made
There's laughter to be had
Growing to be done
Board games to be played

In the mornings, the kitchen will fill
With scented clouds of coffee, freshly made
In reality, there'll be sad times, too
And with a mind like this, no doubt
Those scenes will be replayed and replayed

Yet full, happy hearts will bring the balance
To this central scene in our family life
Where we'll re-find our normal after getting married
The three of us together
Us, officially husband and wife

It's simply bricks and mortar, yes
But it's our family's next chapter
It's the fascinating place from that dream

Brought to life
Ready to be filled with good times
Hard times
Love and growth
Marriage and laughter

It's material things which, this past year
We learned to live without
It's all about making memories
Though the luxuries will add extra comfort
No doubt

This is the happy picture that hung from that chain
In a room full of motion, it was displayed with a slight tilt
It's the home for our family
The memories for our son
It's the house
That Dad built.

WEEK 52

Welcome home – we did it

I was stripped of everything I knew, yet in many ways, my life grew more wholesome than ever before. Now I feel empowered to take on anything that life or motherhood throws at me.

And there we have it – we're in. We started this year in my cosy independent woman nest, not knowing quite where this journey would take us. Now, after almost one year of plasterboard walls, boil-a-baths, and creaking floors, we're in our new home with our baby who I have raised proudly and often single-handedly, in a glorified shed. I'm feeling like quite the woman tonight. We did it and this marks the end of one long, whirling rollercoaster of a transformative year.

Everything in our new home feels still. It's an empty nest, ready to be filled. Rooms with no life are ready to be given character and to soak up the next chapter of our lives, which will one day turn to nostalgia. The bare walls are ready to absorb our energy and the echoes of our conversations – the laughs, the cries, the happy squeals of our baby. These walls will witness him talking, walking, and all the other milestones ahead of us. This home is where I'll continue on my quest to tame the PMDD monster, try different treatments and create a nest for those tumultuous times that thankfully seem much less scary nowadays.

Walking around our finished home has me feeling emotional. I don't know what to do with all this space. Yesterday morning, we moved into our new home and by the afternoon, we'd transformed the kitchen into a winter wonderland for our son's first birthday party. Tonight, he started walking. Tomorrow, he turns one. Amidst this whirlwind, I feel like I've just stepped off a rollercoaster and forgotten to bring my legs with me. As a calm hermit, all I want to do is nest in our new home so I can spend a comforting day on the sofa with Alan Titchmarsh.

There's a long way to go before I can create my new version of those comforting interiors that make me feel like me and soothe my PMDD. It always takes me a long time to settle into a new home, but this past year has taught me that I'm absolutely capable of going back to basics and living a wholesome life – even if that involves uprooting my entire life and home and swapping it for shed life with my firstborn baby. Following this past 52 weeks, I feel like I can do anything. There's nothing like throwing yourself into a metaphorical snowstorm to prove how strong you are. Even still, I'll never take my home comforts for granted again.

Being in our new home brings about a refreshing sense of reality that makes everything before it seem like a dream. Bringing our baby home from hospital; being carried around when I couldn't sit up; meeting all those special people; ditching my mouse squeak and finding my lion's roar; moving into our garden room; bearing with my brain through the desperately low times; bonding with my baby; unleashing my superpowers; embracing our unique living situation; and watching our son grow against the backdrop of our new home being created.

People often repeat the same old sentences at the one-year mark of parenthood, like "where did my baby go?" and "time goes so fast". Instead, my mind is whirling with "what even just happened?" To me, this feels like when you get swept up in the excitement of a holiday and by the time your feet touch home soil, everything feels like a blur. Did we really just live out that year? Brick by brick, our new home was made, whilst day by day, our baby lived his first year and I grew through my first year as a mum. I was stripped of everything I knew, yet in many ways, my life grew more wholesome than ever before. Now I feel empowered to take on anything that life or motherhood throws at me. I wouldn't have had this same confidence, had I not been on this tricky journey.

Throughout my first year of motherhood, I've been thrown into some of the hardest situations of my life. Not only have they helped me to bond with my baby. They've also led me to flourish and highlighted some home truths along the way. Life isn't about having a jaw-dropping nursery, the best holiday on Instagram, or designer baby clothes. Life is about turning to each other when things feel rough, turning your back on the modern world of social media and motherhood-meddlers when it becomes overwhelming and, most of all, turning the mundane moments into an adventure. So, there we have it; the year I became a mum like this. The year I rejected everything the modern world told me I needed, yet I gained more than I could ever imagine.

And There We Have It

And there we have it
My baby's lived his first year
We've had all the emotions
Elated, overwhelmed, scared
Tears over spilt milk
Actual
Real
Tears

I've still not recovered from the birth
My sleep and hormones are all out of whack
Though we rowed our boat through some choppy waters
I've never lived a more wholesome year
Conscious of the precious times we'd never get back

We eased him out of his black and white womb
Into this world exploding with people, colour and light
There's a million things he's learned this year
My favourite one being:
The difference between day and night

I've swapped social media and manic mum-days
For a calm and wholesome approach
That sweet, other worldliness at Vinnies
Those magical vibes of Ginny's
We didn't need a house
Once all this great company became our home

Not forgetting our newest friends
Kerys, you're a special one
Thank you for our memories
I'll forever treasure those
And each candle I light
For the rest of my life
Is for your beautiful baby Rose

The garden room stripped us of our luxuries for a while
We escaped into our reno house during the heatwave
But these adventures brought us closer
Adding extra purpose
More meaning
To our days

My baby lived his first four months in his mum's cosy nest
A perfectly formed palace I built, just for me
The pride cannot be described
Seeing it transform from a home for one
Into two
Then three

I was reluctant to sell that house
I'll admit
Concerned about early motherhood in a shed
But actually
There's no other way I'd have it

That was tricky
Hardest thing I've ever done
But there's nothing like living off-grid
To focus on bonding and making memories
With my son

Everything I thought I couldn't
My baby's proven that I can
Brushing off the contradictory comments
Standing up for myself
Things he'll never remember but, my boy –
I'll tell you when you're a grown man

I grew you
Yet you've grown me
Didn't anticipate that
You've turned my mouse squeak into a lion's roar

Made me realise that
No thanks
I don’t want my pre-baby body back

No need to push you all over social media
My unglazed eyes have watched you grow
This love has diverted the need to scroll
So yes, as promised –
Your hand is *always* held more than my phone

And what a fitting time – tonight, he started walking
Tomorrow, he turns one
Just as we moved from the garden room
Into the house that Dad built
For his fiancée
And his son

Here, we’ll continue to enjoy stories together
Including those about Great-Grandma from Jack Lane
I miss her until the tears burn my face
But I’ll tell her about my forever-boy
When I’m old and grey
And I meet her again

I'm still working on that thicker skin
Setting boundaries makes me calmer
Each negative comment reflects on the speaker
Each setback adds strength to my armour

I used to switch guises
Before I had chance to achieve anything
I'd pluck a project from my head full of dreams
Then just before I finished…
Next round!
Onto the next unfinished thing!

But look what can happen

With a heart full of love
Some work
And a little faith
Everything that was meant for me
Simply found its way

So yes, here we have it
Another dream achieved
There's no way this book would've happened
Without having you
With me

So, here's my cue to sign off
Your first year has been lived
With streaming tears and a heart full of love
I can confidently say…
We did it.

About the author

Laura Rachelle Taylor is an award-winning writer from Cheshire, UK. Her debut book, *A Mum Like This,* is a collection of poetry and prose that explores the demands of modern motherhood through the lens of someone who feels the highs and lows of life with Premenstrual Dysphoric Disorder (PMDD). Laura puts tricky feelings and contradictory topics into relatable words.

Bibliography

1. NHS. 2022. "Alternative methods of feeding your baby: syringe, spoon, cup and bottle feeding." University Hospital Southampton. https://www.uhs.nhs.uk/Media/UHS-website-2019/Patientinformation/Pregnancyandbirth/Alternative-methods-of-feeding-your-baby-3008-PIL.pdf.

2. Torre, Jared B., and Matthew D. Lieberman. 2018. "Putting Feelings Into Words: Affect Labelling as Implicit Emotion Regulation." *Sage Journals* 10, no. 2 (March): 116-124. https://doi.org/10.1177/175407391774270.

3. Heill, Jenna R., and Bruno Bordoni. 2023. "Embryology, Umbilical Cord - StatPearls." NCBI. https://www.ncbi.nlm.nih.gov/books/NBK557490/.

4. Premenstrual Dysphoric Disorder (PMDD): Causes & Treatment." 2023. Cleveland Clinic. https://my.clevelandclinic.org/health/articles/9132-premenstrual-dysphoric-disorder-pmdd.

5. Wadman, Meredith. 2016. "Pregnancy resculpts women's brains for at least 2 years." Science.org. https://www.science.org/content/article/pregnancy-resculpts-women-s-brains-least-2-years.

6. The Rotherham NHS Foundation Trust. 2010. "Antenatal pelvic floor exercises." The Rotherham NHS Foundation Trust. https://www.therotherhamft.nhs.uk/uploadedFiles/Content/Our_Services/Obstetrics_and_Gynaecology/Antenatal%20pelvic%20floor%20exercises(2).pdf.

7. "Why Are We Always Shaming New Mums?" 2018. SheerLuxe. https://sheerluxe.com/life/why-are-we-always-shaming-new-mums.

8. "Bullying now means something different." 2018. BBC. https://www.bbc.co.uk/newsround/44355541.

9. Mustafa, Tanyel. 2021. "81% of mums feel they are judged for how they parent." Metro UK. https://metro.co.uk/2021/05/18/81-of-mums-feel-they-are-judged-over-how-they-parent-14601545/.

10. Holly Ernst. 2019. "How many calories does breastfeeding burn?" Healthline. https://www.healthline.com/health/parenting/breast-feeding-calories#calories-burned.

11. Sinclair, Marlene. 2020. "The wonder world of fetal microchimerism." Ulster University. https://pure.ulster.ac.uk/en/publications/the-wonder-world-of-fetal-microchimerism.

Printed in Great Britain
by Amazon

39948088R00139